ALSO by Christine Stewart-Nuñez

The Poet & The Architect

South Dakota in Poems: An Anthology (Editor)

Bluewords Greening

Untrussed

Scholars and Poets Talk About Queens (Associate Editor)

Action, Influence, Voice: Contemporary South Dakota Women (Co-Editor)

Snow, Salt, Honey

Keeping Them Alive

Postcard on Parchment

Unbound & Branded

The Love of Unreal Things

CHRYSOPOEIA:

Essays of Language, Love, and Place

CHRISTINE STEWART-NUÑEZ

STEPHEN F. AUSTIN STATE UNIVERSITY PRESS

For more information:
Stephen F. Austin State University Press
P.O. Box 13007 SFA Station
Nacogdoches, Texas 75962
sfapress@sfasu.edu

Managing Editor: Kimberly Verhines
Cover Art: Pauline Aitken, *Digitalis versalius*, Digital photomontage. 2006.
Archival pigment print.

Distributed by Texas A&M Consortium
www.tamupress.com

ISBN: 978-1-62288-930-3

First Edition

CONTENTS

For Rochelle

CHRYSOPOEIA:

Essays of Language, Love, and Place

Introduction for Chrysopoeia

Alchemy: The speculative process of transforming experience into knowledge, often through acts of composition: inquire, collect, arrange, reflect, distill.

Inquiry: Déjà vu nags. Dreams recur. I question the text of my own life. Curiosity compels me to smooth out wrinkled memories.

Earth is elemental: Seeds fold into soil and sprout in the warm dark. Shoots push up and out, earthbound yet pulled by heat. Stems become vines and vines become tethers that pulse as they bind. Mountain, prairie, forest, desert, tundra—soil is material foundation. Around earth's greening, we spin and spin and spin.

Collect: A critical mass of messy thought pours from my fingertips: scenes, shimmering details, scraps of dialogue. Magpie-like, I sort and store the shiny bits—charged fragments of experience—before I bring the heat of scrutiny.

Restore: I want to puzzle the past together, one jigsaw after another. I need to fit shard against shard and fuse fractures. And yet time taxes my recollections and raises a host of partial memories—restoration impossible.

Juxtaposition: Analogous to alchemy's chemistry, it's one method of the mix.

Love: If language is the medium, love is the grammar that binds us.

Zodiac: I consult constellations and cards; I seek advice from sacred texts; I ask ancestors; I divine from branches, clouds, and sea spray. What knowledge does my body hold in bones and bile, skin and sweat?

Vulnerability: I am human. I conduct mistakes through symphonies. Silence will not sustain me.

Null: The blank page swept away with a word—a new crucible.

Fire is elemental: With vision, we kindle a spark and the tinder quickens. Cups of flame burst. The sun blazes and moonlight brightens night. Even when light thins to a slice and disappears altogether, even when we can't see with naked eyes the ways the world works, the cycles of moon and sun still coalesce.

Distill: I order to find essential structures. What if I splice? Braid? Follow this segment with that one? Add. Delete. Rearrange. Repeat, repeat, repeat.

Happiness: The distant peaks appear slate, a gradation of color from mountains to white-gray sky and storm clouds. Gray makes a lonely weather; from this, can happiness be stirred by desire? Can it be unearthed, dusted off? I want to believe it's a matter of the mind, that I only need to learn how to free myself instead of waiting for this shock of living on the edge, the moments I'm poised to plummet.

Gold, the Goal: Whether insight is a walnut-sized nugget or the size of a lentil, it's the real deal. Words worth their weight.

Senses are elemental in writing: dates, lemons, olives, almonds, and avocados ready for the tongue; scents of seaside, cedar, smoke, rose, and lilac fill the nose. Touch is temperature and texture and pressure. I persuade with the language of the body.

Unveil: Between geyser steam and glacial ice, the newborn's cry and deceased's last breath; between the ocean's moan and mountain's whistle; between A and Z; between moonrock and lava, ginger and mango; between keening and calm, I tear the scrim.

Kintsukuroi: Japanese artists mend broken pottery with gold and the seams become beautiful. Yet breaking can transform utterly; consider molecules, seed coats, illusions, eggs, cocoons.

Place: Structures, cities, and sites get mapped: beaches, backyards, and bedrooms are coded; houses and hotels, shrines and sculptures, kitchens and train cabins are subject to arrangement; and the forests, cliffs, pubs, parks, ruins, gardens, monuments, and mountains become illuminated with metaphor.

~

Breath & Breeze: Air is elemental. Breath fixes us on this spinning rock, and our lungs inhale ancient atoms. Time collapses, spiral within spiral, as the wind blows. See the dust swirling? Turbines turn above fields brimming with corn, wheat, soybean, sugar beet. Pause, and a breeze will trumpet through our bodies. Breathe, and the rocks will sing.

Opportunity: Sometimes alchemy entails finding opportunity in the midst of confusion. Sometimes it means creating possibilities to shift emotion and perception through imagination.

Metaphor: The magic of imagery colliding with language and creating insight. And sometimes inventing illusion.

Quest: All over my life's map, I'll plant flags of conquest. I'll find the grail, the guy, the gold, the glory. I'll blur the boundaries and erase mistakes. Everything will look clean and clear and conventional at the adventure's end.

Yield: My prayer answered. My brain in paper and heart on a plate. My sound cast out and waiting to land into another's ear, hands, lap.

Xesturgy: Not the polishing of stones but words. Deliberate diction and sentences pared until smooth, they refract light.

Water is elemental: I struggle to splice mist; I wrestle a tsunami's waves; I draw down thunderstorms with fervent prayer; I lace lakes with leisure; I probe the ocean's darkest, coldest places. There's a world of knowledge in a raindrop.

Transmute: To give voice to one's stories and transcend silence.

An Archeology of Secrets

Some ancient Hittite words are very close to their modern English equivalents: for example, the Hittite word for water is *watar* and the word for daughter is *dohter*.

—Shona Grimbly, *Encyclopedia of the Ancient World*

WHEN MY FATHER VISITED me during my two-year teaching stint in Turkey, we never traveled to the capital of the Hittite empire, Hattusas. I'd planned to visit the land of Anatolia controlled by the Hittites in the second millennium BCE. We could've strolled through the Lion Gate with its rain-smoothed cat faces; we might've studied the fortress built from mountain. My father, who'd spent time in the army, would've appreciated the city's strategic place at the southern end of the Budaközü River valley, would've admired the cliffs that protected the city along its north and western borders. The walls surrounding Hattusas, so like a father's arms, almost embraced the city completely.

The Hittites were known only from the Bible—a long dead, perhaps fictional people—until German Assyriologist Hugo Winckler began digging in 1905. By 1910, archeologists uncovered over 10,000 tablet fragments. Experts reported they'd discovered another language, Arzawan, from a previously unknown civilization. They revised this theory when the cuneiform revealed the most archaic form of Indo-European language we have—the language of the Hittites.

In dust-filled quadrants, men hoped for revelation. They recited stories of discovery before them, Troy and Ephesus, and they scraped away clay with faith that centuries of compressed earth would reveal treasures to ground myth in history. Isn't that why we dig? To find language that deciphers who we've been and to connect the pieces of who we may become? So much depends upon a steady hand and the pressure of the pick. One mistake and a potsherd crumbles, its answers disintegrating.

Thirty-five hundred years have passed and two Hittite words remain the same. Not warrior or lover. Not god or coin. Our lips and tongues shape the same sounds, the same *watar*, *dohter*.

THE CONNECTION QUADRANT

> The Hittites blended eastern and western cultures and spread ideas. They ruled over Troy, communicated with the Achaeans, and traded with the Mycenaeans. In Hittite archives scholars have found the first history of Greece— prototypes of Greek myths based on native Anatolian culture as well as some inspired from Hurrian and Mesopotamian models. In essence, the Hittites give us words to prove the historical truths contained within myths.
> —Steve Thurston, "Introduction to the Hittites"

On the first day of his visit, my father and I walked four blocks from my on-campus apartment to a pastry shop. We sat at a circular table-for-two, my father's six-foot frame hunched over a dainty espresso cup. I noticed strands of gray in his otherwise sandy-brown hair. His sea-colored eyes were illuminated by sunlight streaming through the plate glass. On the other side, pedestrians flowed down the sidewalk. Kitty-corner to the pastry shop stood a kiosk where my friends bought cigarettes or the national alcohol, rakı; depending on the season, I bought cherry or carrot juice.

"I have something to tell you," Dad said. His thick fingers grasped the tiny spoon as if it was a child's and we played afternoon tea. As he stirred sugar into the cup, I remembered he usually took his coffee black.

"Is everything okay?" I moved forward in my chair. Was he ill? Was my mother? Did my younger brother get in some sort of trouble?

"I have another daughter." Each word sounded hesitant, smuggled, as if his brain delivered the syllables to his lips, but his tongue refused to unwrap them.

I opened my mouth to speak. The sounds of honking and gear-grinding cars battered us when the shop door opened. Customers pressed chatter around us. Dad stared at the bag hanging off the back of my chair.

Two emotions coursed through my body. The first, betrayal. *An affair?* I caught my breath and remembered my mother coping with years of his heavy drinking and the death of my sister, Theresa. *That can't be it*, I thought. I couldn't quite comprehend it; this kind of secret bubbled up over coffee and baklava with friends, not fathers. The second, elation. *A flesh-and-blood sister?* I imagined shopping trips, manicures, makeovers.

"How old is she? Where does she live? Have you met her? What is her name?"

"Vicki. She's thirty-four. Wisconsin." I did the math and sat back in my chair, astonished. *She's the same age as Theresa would be now*, I thought. "I went up there a few weeks ago," Dad continued. "I knew she was my daughter the moment I saw her." His voice quavered, a slip of tone I recognized from the morning I woke up to sirens. Dad was standing on the porch, his flannel robe pulled around him. When I'd asked what was happening, he only whispered, "They can't find her pulse." Theresa was dead at twenty years old from carbon monoxide poisoning—ruled an accident because she was drunk.

But now, Vicki, this new sister sprung fully grown from his head as if Athena.

THE REVELATION QUADRANT

> The public knows little about the Hittites. Studying Biblical archeology and ancient Egypt tends to have more appeal; furthermore, for centuries "history itself conspired to erase them." Much of the little information that is known is old, out of date, and wrong. Recent scholarship has sought to change that.
>
> —Steve Thurston, "Introduction to the Hittites"

One afternoon, when I was sixteen, my mother and I sat at my grandparents' kitchen table finishing lunch. The lights were off to keep the trailer cool. We sipped iced tea, drops of condensation sliding off the glasses and pooling on the plastic tablecloth. The sentences between my mother and grandmother slowed, suspended in the sticky August air. I dozed until my grandmother mentioned the time she almost left the Catholic Church. She sniffed, a sign the circumstances still bothered her. I spent the next hour wondering, too polite to press for details.

"What was so earth-shattering that Grandma and Grandpa almost left the Church?" I asked as soon as my mom and I were out the door.

Mom slid into the car and rolled down the windows. The "whole truth" had always been important to her. "A half-truth," she said once, "might as well be a lie." For a moment she seemed to consider her answer.

"Your father and I didn't get married until Theresa was sixth months old. Our parish priest tried to convince me to give her up for adoption even though I planned to keep her." She stared at the road as she pulled onto the street, her hand white-knuckled on the steering wheel. "My parents supported me. Angry about the priest's insistence, they almost left the Church."

I exhaled. Finally! My mother—a person with a dramatic past. I was proud of her refusal to surrender to a bully, but I couldn't imagine my grandparents fighting outright with the priest.

Still, I had a question, not well-chosen but too important for my teenage mind to ignore.

"So do Theresa and I have the same dad?'

"Of course you do," Mom responded, her tone a blend of hurt and indignation. She stopped at a light and signaled left. She kept her eyes on the road.

"Cool," I said, relieved I didn't have to adjust to this other new truth. "You were really strong for what you did." I continued after a pause, "Thanks for telling me."

For years we never spoke of it again.

THE CONFLICT QUADRANT

> The Hittites mastered the use of an innovative lightweight chariot, which contributed significantly to their rise to power in Anatolia and Syria even when threatened by Egypt. Pulled by two small horses, the chariot had three advantages: it was fast, mobile, and could be used as an archery, javelin, and spear platform.
>
> —Steve Thurston, "Introduction to the Hittites"

"How come you didn't know about Vicki until recently?" I asked my father, forking a piece of baklava. He shifted in his seat.

"Her mother was married," he answered.

Complicated possibilities thundered across the field of my father's past and I could feel his heart—and mine—beat faster. Among the scenes taking flight in my imagination, one spiraled through the air and landed at my feet: my father, age twenty-one, flirting with the beauties who sat in his salon chair. Dad would compliment a woman's thick tresses as he set her hair in rollers or teased her locks into a beehive. His hand lingered on her shoulder. Married or not, they'd always blush.

He'd been a star stylist. The salon owner was grooming him to manage a new store. Instead, around the time of Theresa's birth, he got drafted. Mom said the anatomy classes Dad took in beauty school qualified him to train as a medic at Fort Leavenworth, Kansas. In 1965 he helped set up an evacuation hospital in Vietnam. In six months, hands that had cut bangs for women in miniskirts began to sew up the wounds of soldiers.

No photos of my father in-country exist, so I must imagine him sitting at a table amid flea market booths with thatched roofs. Behind him, women in wide hats sell fish. His right hand holds a gray rice bowl, the other grips a can of "tiger piss," a word they used for beer. His medic shirt hugs his broad shoulders and the upturned cuff reveals the blue edge of a tattoo. An army jacket, thrown over the chair, matches the blanket he brought home—the camouflaged one good for making forts. His smile isn't reserved like the one in his wedding photo, but his crewcut is the same. Buddies sit around him—two Aussies who joined the war to drink and a New Yorker with his arm around a Korean marine.

I imagine the top of a pen inside his jacket, its gold cap clipped over a pocket. It's the pen he used to sign the letters Mom told me about. He wrote to dead guys' wives and parents detailing the days he spent at their loved one's side. He took dictation from a guy whose hand got blown off. He penned a few love letters, too.

When he got home, he didn't perm hair or clean scalpels again. On June 6, 1966 he started working on the line at a factory that made airplane parts for fighter jets and commercial carriers. He worked for that company until he retired.

THE STORY QUADRANT

Anatolian art between 1650 and 1200 BCE fails to reveal creative flair or technical accomplishment. Described as naturalistic, a Hittite artist seemed to strive to render an object's essence. The principal purpose of Hittite art is to evoke feeling rather than to portray fact.

—J.G. Macqueen, *The Hittites and Their Contemporaries in Asia Minor*

The third day of our trip my father and I drove west along the Mediterranean Sea to a nice beach. I fantasized about an Oprah-style reunion with Vicki based on the few details I'd discovered: she was blonde and blue-eyed, and her daughter was too. According to Dad, Mom was okay with the news. She'd always known it might be a possibility, but never imagined a daughter surfacing after all this time.

With the seawater too cold to take more than a quick dip, Dad and I brought our paperbacks down to the beach and arranged towels on lounge chairs. Never had I witnessed my father read a novel. I stared at the gentle way he turned the pages. When he lowered the book and gazed out at the sea, I followed his eyes.

"Those ruins out there were built about a thousand years ago as part of a fortification plan for this area," I said, pointing to the squat turrets and walls on an island a good swim's distance away. My friends and I made it out there once, but the swim exhausted me and there wasn't much on the island except sharp rocks. "It's called Kiz Kalesi," I said. "Girl's Castle."

"Why's that?" Dad asked. He studied the castle for a few minutes without speaking. Everything seemed simple—blank sky, light breeze, soft expression on my father's face.

"According to legend, soon after the birth of a princess, a fortune teller told the king his daughter would die from a snakebite. To protect his daughter, the king cloistered her in the castle, but an asp snuck into a basket of grapes brought to feed the princess."

A shift. My father's eyes narrowed; his jaw tightened.

"Interesting story." He sat up and pointed to an outdoor café just beyond the sand. "Will those waiters serve beer on the beach?"

Sober since Theresa died, he'd ordered a beer the evening he told me about Vicki. My colleagues had ordered beers at dinner, too, so I thought he did just to go along. The next day he ordered two. During our day soaking up heat on the beach, he drank all afternoon.

THE THEORIZING QUADRANT

Hittite prayer reflects the culture's straightforward philosophy of life and the interdependency of life and death: "Man is mortal, and man is sinful. Even if a man is himself innocent, the sins of his father fall upon him; he is afflicted by sickness and misery. But when a man cries to a god for mercy the god listens."

—J.G. Macqueen, *The Hittites and Their Contemporaries in Asia Minor*

During my childhood, I feared the sound of a shot glass clinking on a countertop, the ensuing glaze of my father's silence. How many nights had I stood outside the bathroom door while he puked up pork chops?

I was eight when I walked up the stairs, linoleum still shiny, and saw Dad at the kitchen table. His t-shirt was starched by sweat and a hammer hung from a loop in his mud-streaked jeans. In the light of the television, he forked roast beef left-handed, his right wrist swollen, immobile. His puffy face looked as if he'd been in a fist fight. Blood patched his skin from hand to elbow. A couple cases of beer had helped him re-shingle our roof. Theresa, dressed in her nurse's aide uniform, stood with her hands on her hips. She saw me and stomped out. Had they been fighting again? Did she say something was broken? With my arms wrapped around my stomach, I shuffled closer. Rainbow-hued, his skin, the colors of my crayons: yellow-green, cornflower, violet. I reached out, wanting to touch him.

"Daddy, I said. "What's wrong?" Did I mean with his wrist? Did I want an answer to why Theresa left? What words did I expect?

"Nothing."

He tried to scoop up mashed potato with his left hand, working to keep pain off his face, then turned back to the ten o'clock news.

THE DECIPHERING QUADRANT

Bedřich Hrozný, a young Czech, "re-discovered" Hittite by deciphering rhymed lines: "NU NINDA-AN EZZATENI WATAR-MA EKUTENI." He knew the Babylonian sign for bread, "ninda", and deduced "ezza" to mean "eat." Its potential as a cognate of the Greek "edein", Latin "edere" and German "essen" followed. Other words leapt out— "nu": now, "watar": water: "Now you will eat bread and drink water."
            —Christian Falvey, "Bedřich Hrozný – Re-Discoverer
                of the Hittite Language"

Toward the end my father's visit, we ate at a tourist restaurant in Cappadocia built inside a hollowed-out cave. To entertain diners, it featured dances associated with Turkish culture. I felt silly walking into a rock wearing heels and a dress, but once inside, the cement sidewalk turned into a plush red carpet. Clarinet, drum, and saz players performing traditional Turkish music greeted us.

The host seated us at a circular table and continued to add other guests. Between plates of rice wrapped in grape leaves and stuffed peppers, we watched a Turkish wedding folk dance: a woman with red, transparent scarves swept over her face married a young farmer, the gold jewelry gifted to them jingling as they danced. After bread stuffed with cheese and creamy yogurt mixed with garlic and cucumbers, we watched six Sufi mystics whirl in the Dervish tradition. While the waiters replaced our empty plates with a tray of grilled lamb and chicken—and refilled my father's empty wine glass—we watched belly-dancers shimmy and swirl.

I noticed, toward the end of the evening, my father's red-cheeked flush. When he reached to top off his glass of wine, I opened my mouth. *What are you doing?* I wanted to ask, thirsting for the reason he picked up the bottle again. He caught my eye and looked away. Suddenly I was exhausted. My leg began to bounce under the table and I glanced at my watch.

"Let's get going," I said.

"I'm not done yet," he replied.

When he was, we walked back to the hotel in silence. I was sitting on one of the twin beds in our room when I recognized his characteristic scowl. A wild card. It could mean he would skulk the rest of the evening and I could tiptoe around him to avoid provoking his anger. Or it could be a clue that he's unhappy and that he's sorting through his thoughts. Or that he's simply drunk. Or, or, or.

"Before we leave I'm going to buy one of those tables," I said, breaking the silence. "The kind with mother-of-pearl inlay on the collapsible legs. I like the table top I saw today. All are circular and metal, but not all are etched the same way." I regretted my decision as soon as the sentences left my lips.

"How much will you pay for it?" he sneered. Spending money was too much pressure.

"About a hundred dollars," I said, fishing for my toothbrush in my bag.

"Why spend so much on something like that?" He kept his body turned askew, yet he managed to look at me over his shoulder, his eyebrows pressed together.

"They're over-priced here because this is a tourist area, but I can't find them in Tarsus and I'll be coming home in three months."

His snarl meant *You're a fool.* He turned his back to me and pretended to sleep. I grabbed my calling card and headed out to find a phone.

I don't know how long I wandered around empty streets. When I found a canary-yellow public telephone, I leaned into the privacy of its metal arms. The phone rang and rang.

"Mom," I said when she picked up. "Dad's drinking again." I sobbed into the receiver. "It started out with a few beers. Now he's drinking several glasses of wine at dinner, too." Thirteen years of sobriety ruined by his trip to see me. I felt ready to vomit.

"Let's not worry about it unless he keeps it up," Mom said. "It's not your fault, okay?" I calmed down. Perhaps this was only temporary. Perhaps, if he never saw me drink, he wouldn't drink again. Perhaps if I never brought it up, I could squeeze out the beer and wine from my sunbaked shell of memory.

THE HOPE QUADRANT

> The Hittites, who may have invented the treaty, used them to secure their empire and justify their political domination. "When the Hittites wanted war, the Near East was at war, and when the Hittites wanted peace, the Near East was at peace. When they collapsed, it marked the end of The Bronze Age."
>
> —Steve Thurston, "Introduction to the Hittites"

My dad and I drove three hours east of Tarsus to Urfa to see the Sacred Carp Pool. Children stood around its edges and sprinkled pellets into the water. The food drew carp through the pond's surface like silver ribbons. Sacred, the fish are wood-turned-flesh by Jehovah, a miracle that saved Abraham from death at the stake while preaching to the unconverted Mesopotamians. The fire turned to water.

The peaceful beauty of the site impressed me. Pilgrims wearing embroidered velvet dresses and decorated headscarves filled the stone-cut courtyard and the women whispered to each other as they drew water from a sacred well. I wanted to believe in the miracle of water, fish, and fire—the power of immediate and lasting transformation—just as I had believed Theresa's death was powerful enough to cause my father to quit drinking.

A secret, at the beginning, starts out as an inconsistency in the architecture of a life. Today, when my mother calls to tell me that my inebriated father has fallen on the sidewalk—scraping his face, spraining his wrist, losing his glasses—I will imagine the elaborate defenses he constructs to conceal his drinking—the oddly timed errands, the thermos filled with vodka. I, too, build a fortress of diversions to protect the shadow-sides of my life. But the secret is always revealed. Someone digs around and uncovers it. Or the façade is simply too exhausting to maintain.

Walls crumble under the pressure of time. Modern archeologists leave some quadrants in a dig untouched; someday, tools will calibrate the right amount of pressure, and nothing will be lost. Until then, we work with fragments of history and piece together what we can.

Watar, dohter. Language decoded; gaps, slips, silences recognized. How much work did it take to decipher two simple words? I grasp at hope: I want to be the daughter that didn't die young, the daughter that didn't disappoint by only wanting money after all those years of silence, the daughter whose existence inspires a reconciliation between stories currently unfolding and the fragments of the past.

Writers of Calendars

"PLEASE, GRANDMA, RECORD YOUR STORIES." I placed a plain-lined notebook in her hands.

She looked as if ready to speak but put the notebook on the table. In three days, I'd leave to work in Turkey, and I sensed the opportunity to clarify how I—the poet and adventurer—fit into my family was slipping away. The oldest in her family married to the oldest in my grandfather's, Grandma was the brightest star in the Lenan/Grafton constellation. And somehow I knew she would die before I completed my two-year teaching contract. Lunch-time naps, a clutch of pill bottles, and doctor appointments inked onto her calendar spoke over her silence.

She was barely five feet tall. Once, weight had gathered at her waist. Now cancer loosened her blue-knit pants and muddled the tenderness in her hazel eyes. I picture her leaning against the kitchen counter, beige twinset fancied up with a beaded necklace and rhinestone clip-ons. She wears her black hair, heavily streaked with silver, short and permed. Tapping a pen in a calendar's margin, she checks on the week's events and considers yesterday's weather. In these grids she connects clusters of light—family in California, Missouri, Arkansas, and Colorado—by birth, anniversary, and death dates. She pockets the pen and she heads out for church. A faint blend of Aqua Net and scented talcum powder hangs in the air.

Without me to coax the sentences onto the page, Grandma never filled the notebook. Between treatments she pressed sentences in correspondence and squeezed words into her daily calendar. While she was dying on another continent, I composed alliterative phrases about the Turkish landscape and pieced together images from our lives.

JUNE 2008

With the afternoon sun to her back, Mom walked into my house in South Dakota with an overnight bag in one hand and a Wal-Mart sack stuffed to a breaking point in the other.

"I'd thrown these into the trash," she said, setting the sack near me with a soft thud. "Then I took them out in case you wanted them." She pushed the sack to me. Through the transparent film, I saw faint, compressed cursive: round Os, Ds, and Bs slimmed to ovals; lowercase Ls thinned to uncrossed Ts.

"I'd forgotten about these," I said, running my finger along a calendar's spiraled edge. For over two decades, minus an occasional week, Grandma wrote about each day's events in a two-by-two-inch box. "Why do you think she kept calendars?"

"Perhaps she was a writer like you," Mom replied. I noticed our similar script, messy and cramped within lines as if written between tree rings. I sensed her hand gravitating to paper as mine does, the urgent note scrawled next to a full moon symbol as if written to unveil words. I felt the pressure of a pen, the hardened callous bump under the tissue of skin.

"Then why didn't she keep a diary—something more expansive?"

Mom looked up from the sink where she was washing her hands. "Maybe this was the best she could do."

SEPTEMBER 1996

I traveled to Mount Nemrut in the Adıyaman province on Grandma's birthday, September 22, to see the tomb of Antiochus I. As I loaded my backpack into a minivan at dusk and sandwiched myself between colleagues for an eight-hour ride east from Tarsus, Grandma was probably enjoying a lunch of egg salad with Grandpa. We traveled along pistachio groves—a long stretch of landscape without streetlights or towns. The air cooled and became drier. Grandma's calendar doesn't reveal details, but I imagine she celebrated her birthday at the Golden Corral Buffet. That night as I slept, swaying with the moving minivan, she sliced through spice cake and sipped a mug of decaf.

We arrived at Mount Nemrut, the resting place of the king who had ruled Commagene from 70 B.C.E. to 38 B.C.E., at dawn. Stiff and groggy, we stumbled out of the van and gathered outside a tea-shack.

A man placed warm glasses in our hands and we waited for the sky to turn gray on the eastern horizon. I seemed to shrink under the star-studded sky. I pulled the sleeve of my wool sweater over my hand against the cold, wishing I had brought my journal. Moonlight illuminated the gravel-topped tomb. Here, Antiochus may have celebrated Pompey's confirmation of him as king; here, he may have scoffed at Mark Antony's attempt to fine him for neglecting to aid a Roman ally. Here, he existed beyond the fragments of Roman record-keeping at the center of his own royal cult. Future generations would hike to this mountain with offerings.

In the zone between sleep and wakefulness, I gazed at the multitude of stars. Had I ever seen a night so thick with light? My mind swung from stars to memories of stars: sitting on Grandma's porch steps and penciling in my diary; walking through an autumn field of papery cornstalks, the moon heavy overhead. Wrapped in the humidity of a Midwest summer and cooled by the arid mountain air, the scent of tea brought me firmly into the present. The mountain stretched up ahead, the tea warm in my hands.

JULY 2008

Two weeks passed before I looked at the calendars carefully. Alone in my kitchen, laptop screen glowing and tea steeping, I paused. What would I find in these windows to the past? My hands peeled back the plastic as if the contents, exposed to direct light, could evaporate. I stuck my nose in the sack. Mildew. One calendar was bolted to cardboard, gray spores on one side, faded gold writing on the other: "Modern Optical. 206 Euclid, Des Moines, Iowa." Underneath, in red: "March 1974. The sure sign of the little man is the big head."

I held the calendar in my hand; Grandma must have touched the calendar like this when she moved it from underneath the green rotary telephone. This month Grandma recorded birthdays in her shorthand: On Tuesday, March 12: "Thomas Wayne (Tony) G. 22," indicating that Grandpa's brother, Tony Grafton, was born in 1922. I lifted the damp page. March 21: "Bake pie for dinner at church." April 5: "Theresa and Sharon, 1:30." This was somewhat unusual because my mother and sister's visit was recorded in my mother's handwriting. I imagine Grandma standing back from a month to connect all the visits, birthdays, and bake sales, the line shaping story.

I flipped through other calendars. What did she want to remember when she wrote "Chris back from Europe" on June 28, 1993? Did these fragments help her access memories like they did for me? Recording names and bits of detail—the quality of sunshine, the kind of baked deliciousness she made for church—became evidence of important events. And she also created opportunities to make memories. Perhaps writing down the day I was due back from Europe reminded her to keep the afternoon free to accompany my parents to the airport.

I recall the two of us pouring over photos of Belgium, ticket stubs from Paris museums, a map of my favorite Vienna neighborhood, and an unsent postcard of Florence. She had always wished to go to Italy where my grandfather spent time in World War II, but family responsibilities kept her home. I read bits from my journal aloud: "Tried to find the Piazza de Michelangelo. Ate pasta with pesto at a café with flower-stenciled mirrors, peeling white paint, exposed red bricks. Met Rosario, a Sicilian stubborn enough to pursue a three-hour conversation with me by working through a phrasebook." Toward the end of my photograph pile, Grandma brought out a few photos of Grandpa in Italy and a gift box. Out of the wrinkled "Made in Italy" cardboard, she lifted a shell ring: Grandma's image in a tiny cameo on its face.

SEPTEMBER 1996

With more light, we hiked the short but steep path. Pulverized rock crunched under our boots. On the east-facing terrace we watched the sun paint a gold veneer on miles and miles of pocked earth. Antiochus must have seen a lush landscape where the sky poured itself into the Upper Euphrates, a shimmering thread of prosperity. The breadbasket of the ancient world. I thought of Grandma in the new breadbasket, the American Midwest. That month, when I opened her letter—three pages of thin, almost translucent paper—I expected the script stretched across the guiding lines to dissolve before I read it: "Hi honey! I haven't forgotten you, but so many things happened. We went to Branson for a week—didn't see any shows but did a little shopping. Your grandpa caught lots of fish. We will be eating fish all winter."

Her letters dulled my homesickness yet disappointed me. I wanted engaging remembrances of her family's life on the farm; I longed for details of my grandfather's latest carpentry project, probably a stepstool crafted to look like a turtle. Still, hand-written in blue ink, the same color of my teapot and the saltshaker on my kitchen counter, her letters felt intimate. In slices of the quotidian she gave me the events that inspired concern or joy. I looked at the moonscape, the ashen crust of earth, and gathered the images to describe in a letter. So much was unspoken between us—her dreams for me, my desire to see more clearly the silences implied in the bits of anecdotes she shared.

JULY 2008

I skimmed over a few calendars before I realized I was looking for a specific date: 1984. Snippets filled that fall: "Went to Penney [J.C. Penney's] & R.G. [Richman Gordman's] with Ruth." "Theresa here between classes" on two Wednesdays in September, the start of her third year of college. In October, my uncle ate breakfast with them almost every day. November eighth: "Theresa here." I realized, with tenderness, how often my sister visited them. The following weekend, Grandma shopped both days. And the twelfth, the day before Theresa dies: "20° 6 a.m." My eyes began to sting. When I saw what she wrote on November 13, a "T" followed by a line through every day until the twenty-second of November, I broke into tears.

During one of those silent days, I tiptoed to Theresa's casket. I tucked letters between her suede skirt and the satin coffin lining. The funeral home was cold, so cold. With each breath, the scent of chrysanthemums, lilies, and roses nauseated me. A rosary draped across Theresa's hands. Her opal ring, catching the light from the dimmed spotlights above her, sparkled. I caressed the mini carnations on a satin pillow and I smoothed out the ribbon inscribed with "Beloved Sister."

During one of those silent days, I wrote a poem about a dying rose. A clichéd metaphor of life cut down. In my poem, I planted the rose's seeds. Somehow, at eleven years old, I believed I'd find meaning in her death. From this point, I'd write to record and to think through emotions with metaphors and images. Words comforted me. They connected ideas, created space and light to walk by.

Grandma drew a line through nine days. A flat line of death, a slice through her life. A crack creating fragments. Did she see her line as a metaphor? Or was she drawn to the calendar, pen in hand, only to find she couldn't write words? Why, even after the week of guests and the

Friday funeral, did Grandma not write? Perhaps grief disrupted her routines; perhaps, suddenly, the temperature seemed inconsequential; perhaps she didn't want to remember these days of unyielding sorrow. She tended to her daughter and grandchildren. Eventually, life resumed. And she continued her calendars.

Maybe Mom was right. Calendars were Grandma's form, her genre, because that was all she knew. She was a keeper of stories who never had the opportunity to learn the nuances of telling them. Her father forbade her to go to college because he believed education wasn't appropriate for women; she married at an age much later than her peers and soon birthed two children. When my mom and uncle became school-aged, Grandma worked to earn money to send them to Catholic school, which she deemed the better educational choice. As writers, both of us compressed stories into phrases, but as I practiced, I added to my repertoire: scene, reflection, figurative language. Proud of my accomplishments, she posted my poems on her refrigerator, but complicating that pride was another emotion. Was it wistfulness? Frustrated desire transformed, over several decades, to acceptance?

SEPTEMBER 1996

I wandered alone amid the larger-than-life stone sculptures on the terraces of Mount Nemrut. Once these statues flanked the tumulus standing nearly ten meters high, but earthquakes toppled them. More light revealed details of Antiochus's religious lineage: his own statue, clean-shaved and crowned with a royal headdress; Zeus with a massive curly beard and a warrior's helmet; Mithraic Apollo, the god of light and darkness and the most important to Antiochus.

One stone block depicted an astrological calendar, a lion with a crescent over his mane, the stars on his body representing Mars, Venus, and Jupiter. It bears Antiochus's coronation date: 62 B.C.E. Antiochus commissioned calendars depicting constellations—his own esoteric astrology—because he envisioned a religious legacy for his kingdom, slivers of which survive. One scholar argues that Christians refined the Mithraic initiation ceremony—practiced by Antiochus—as baptism. I imagine the cosmic nod to Antiochus that occurred when the priest sprinkled Grandma, Theresa, and me with water to mark the moments we were cleansed, linked by religion and blood.

Walking amid the colossal heads, I maneuvered over the fragments of stones, the pedestals of crumbled sculptures. I stroked the broad-nosed lions meant to protect the gods and give them strength. Like the other tourists, I turned to the sun when the pinkening sky changed the eagle's curved beak from gray to gold.

OCTOBER 2008

I sat at my kitchen table describing the "shimmering surface" of Antiochus's calendars and studying a torn piece of paper—a poem I wrote for Grandma about Mount Nemrut. Shifting my chair to the proper angle, I gazed out at the green-turning-yellow leaves of a birch and into the beige buildings of Tarsus crowding out a wider view of the town: the bazaar next to an excavated Roman road, the two-thousand-year-old public baths, cement houses connected by trellises of jasmine and vines of morning glory. Phrases for a new poem flowed between the remembered shouts of students as they poured out of the campus gates. As I held the fragments of Grandma's days and the images of Antiochus's tomb up to the light, studying their textures, edges, and compressions of time, I saw how necessary it feels to find meaning and record it for the future. By the time I had finished the poem, the buses in my memory started up and sputtered away, and the wind began to shake a few leaves off the trees. Soon it would be November.

Hike to the Black Madonna

THE ACHING MUSCLES OF MY CALVES began to tremble just as the forest broke away. A white river threaded the valley floor far below. I turned to the right and above the tips of pine emerged the Sümela Monastery. This windowed building of six stories—seamlessly carved out of sheer rock—opened to the sky, its arched doorways shrouded in cloud I had perceived as mist from far below.

In 1930, a fire gutted the library, guest rooms, courtyards, church, and monk housing. It was only seven years after the new Turkish government relocated local Orthodox Greeks to Greece. Among the skeletal wall-remains, 1200 meters above sea level, tourists appeared and disappeared; secured to their heads were hardhats the color of lemons, an illusion of safety amid falling rock and slippery walkways.

The clash of the mountain panorama and cliff-side building amplified as I walked among the monastery's dissolving walls. Graffiti-carved names—Nurten, Yavir, and Nebile—looked like words of prayer. On the interiors of some walls, sun and wind peeled the pain off frescoes even as I studied them. Cut out sections revealed layers of plaster over rough stone. Vandals gouged out saints' eyes on paintings within arm's reach. In one, too high for violence, the hand of Jesus compelled Lazarus's body from an open tomb. And was this Mary, head halo-wrapped, body cloaked in red? At her center, the infant Jesus holding his arms out in blessing. The walls of my childhood church seemed to rise up, and I felt awe just as I did praying before the fourth station of the cross, the priest's words, *Jesus meets his mother*, in my ears.

I stood within these stories overwhelmed by an interior of debris: desire, conception, death, and resurrection held together in stone even as that stone decayed. How was I to know then that the icon—the Black Madonna—serene in her wall niche, was missing? Mary and I gazed at each other with serious eyes, and I searched through a jumble of stories, time and space blurring—a choice to look for the woman inside.

TRABZON: OUR SCHOOL'S-OUT DESTINATION. Neither Chad, my boyfriend, nor I had traipsed across northeastern Turkey yet. With my two-year teaching stint in Tarsus complete, I planned to unwind from an exhausting semester before returning to the States for graduate school. Only halfway through his contract, Chad would be back in Turkey in August. I hoped our time alone would strengthen our relationship before the "long distance" phase.

We walked across tarmac toward a twenty-seater airplane, scarlet-lettered *Bodrum* emblazoned upon its white paint.

"That's hilarious. We're flying to Trabzon in the *Bodrum*," I said to Chad, reaching for his hand. A colleague had nicknamed Bodrum "Bed Room:" a place to swim, barhop, and seduce tourists. "It's like flying to Las Vegas in the *Chastity*. Instead of beaches and bars, we'll be touring Orthodox churches."

He smiled and slung his arm around my backpack.

I pictured the Sümela Monastery, named for a Greek word stemming from "dark" or "black." Later I would learn about the Black Madonna icon and ponder the incongruity of her slender, European nose and thin lips with her black hair and dark skin. Like all Black Madonnas, her contrasting features inspired conjecture. Centuries of stories, deposited within the vessel of Mary's body, shifted over time.

Chad sighed and stretched out, staring at the seatback in front of him. I read this as preoccupation, as invitation to initiate conversation. Nearby a passenger shoved a duffel bag into an overhead bin; others squeezed themselves between armrests. I pulled out the seat belt and buckled it across my waist.

"Hey. I'm sure I'm not," I said to Chad. "I shouldn't have mentioned I was late until I knew for sure. But if you keep being worried, you'll make me worried." I tried to catch his eye.

"We're always safe, but you said you're never this late." Did he think

I was lying? "Let's not talk about this right now." He pulled out a book from his bag.

The flight attendant's wedding ring glinted as she set the tea down on a lap tray. I plunked a sugar cube into my glass, a tiny vase curved like a woman's body. The grains of sugar broke free and floated up before merging into the sienna-colored tea. One of my hands drifted to my flat belly, the other to the rim of the glass.

"It's probably stress," I said. "If I don't obsess about it, it'll come. Besides, this is our *vacation*. Just the two of us."

His answer: a squeeze of my hand before opening the book.

I interpreted this as affirmation. As I sipped the steaming tea, my mind turned the kaleidoscope of possibilities. A half-inch twist changed the geometric slips of paper—me, Chad, school, one year's time—from a mandala of jewels into an aqua and russet burst, one version of the story. Another? Twelve years of Catholic school burned The Visitation behind my eyes. I imagine Mary's hair as the color of walnuts. Cooking lamb, she tucks a stray curl under her hair covering and lapses into a daydream about a cute neighbor. Gabriel drops by; her kaleidoscope turns.

"God's tapped you," the angel explains. "What do you say?" She's given a choice and thinks about it, but scripture doesn't convey silence well. Her "yes" inverts the shape of her future. She could've said no.

Minus the angel and miraculous conception, I thought when faced with pregnancy, I'd watch mirrors and light blur the colors before me. I'd search for an answer within.

WITH NO SUMMIT OF THE ZIGANA MOUNTAINS to inspire us yet, Chad and I trekked the path snaking through the forest. The saturated air infused each deep breath with the scent of pine and slowed my pace. Tight from travel, my muscles strained to push, and I negotiated the curves of the steep ascension with care. Chad's muscles, remembering thousands of bouldering hikes, propelled him with ease. After an hour, my t-shirt and jeans stuck to my skin; I wished I had braved shorts despite the stares of disapproval I'd receive. The narrowed eyes of men always conjured fragments of a memory: a man's hand on my shoulder; a wall closing in; my fingers squeezing his throat; his feet hitting pavement. I still breathed through the anger and fear summoned by memories of this attempted attack. With my blonde hair and blue eyes, had he assumed I was a "Natasha"—a Russian sex worker?

Our steps regularized as the forest thickened, the canopy of leaves shielding us from direct sun. Partway up Chad and I veered off the main trail and followed an overgrown dirt path. It ended at ruins. On a chunk of stone we rested, sipping from our water bottles. The smell of the crumbling house—two partial walls and pile of stacked rubble—was a blend of mold and piss. Perhaps this dwelling had once sheltered pilgrims seeking Sümela's sacred springs. According to legend, the Black Madonna asked angels to remove her icon from Athens where Saint Luke had sent his painting. Mary chose this mountain and she created a place of healing.

Back on the dusty trail, I focused on my walking sandals, one step in front of the other. Every few minutes I caught a glimpse of a brown trunk swathed in moss or a branch veiled in leaves of translucent green, each leaf a halo of light.

CHAD AND I HAD TROUBLE finding a hotel in Trabzon. On the outside we were tourists—good business—but once hotel clerks opened our Turkish work permits (they designated our status as teachers which often meant cheaper prices) and studied the inside, they read a different story. The permit marked us "single," but we asked for one room. They scrutinized me, listening to my clumsy Turkish. "No vacancy," they finally said, snapping the permits shut.

I doubted them. The number of Natashas in Trabzon reinforced their stereotypes of non-Turkish women. I had become accustomed to, although never comfortable with, Turkish men glancing at my short blonde hair and asking me for sex. Walking home from the market, a sack of tomatoes and carrots in my arms, I would pass a small group of men leaning against a wall and smoking cigarettes. Avoiding eye contact that might "invite" a remark, I stared at the back of women's tight ponytails or fringed headscarves. I imagine one of the smokers noticed my hair first. He probably elbowed his friend. Taking a drag of his cigarette, he would exhale: "Hello, Natasha" followed by a flurry of Turkish. The first month I blushed; the second I glared even though it amused them. When their "Hey, Natasha, Natasha" faded, my neck relaxed, shoulders softened, and pace slowed. I marched faster if one followed me for several blocks. I tried to ignore the ways men interpreted my exterior, the narratives they assumed from the color of my hair and eyes.

We secured a hotel after two proprietors refused us. Nestled among a series of red-shingled businesses, Hotel Nur topped a deeply sloping street. Two steep flights of stairs ended with our room. Once inside the door, Chad took four steps and stood in front of a nightstand between twin beds. The angle of light, streaming from a window, illuminated the thickness of his body, corded muscles from rock climbing softened by slight cushioning—the result of his own great cooking. I dropped my backpack on the right bed and pushed open the only other door. The closet-sized bathroom was just the right size for saint's niche. I could imagine Mary Magdalene—from a fresco featured in my guidebook—smoothing out her hair in the mirror. Her elongated fingers and neck, pale cheeks, and somber expression created a version of this woman I didn't recognize; I always imagined her as curvy, a bit plump even, with knowing eyes, thick, loose hair, and a slight smile on her lips.

Only my head reflected in the mirror above the basin as I washed my hands and face. When I opened the door, Chad stood there, a pregnancy test in his hand.

"Where'd you get this?" I asked, touching the corner of the box.

"Lisa had one and gave it to me before we left."

My hand recoiled. "You told her?" I wondered how many other friends knew about this possibility. Suddenly, my stomach flip-flopped.

"Yeah, well I was worried that you'd be worried."

"I'm not," I replied, folding my arms in front of me.

I PUT OFF THE TEST by suggesting dinner. At the restaurant a case of fresh *alabalık* laid out on crushed ice greeted us, reminding me of my father's autumn catches of trout in the cold streams of northern Iowa. We pointed to two we wanted and ordered tomato and cucumber salad, pita, and lentil soup. I placed a napkin over the head of my fish; its blank, watching eye bothered me as I separated meat from bones. Chad chatted about his plans to leave in three days for the States. I would travel alone for another week before meeting a friend in Istanbul and sightseeing for two weeks with her.

"Do you have to go back this week? Maybe you could change your departure date and go back when I meet Melissa."

"That would be impossible. I've been planning a summer of mountain-climbing and beer-drinking for months."

I don't remember the rest of our conversation or if there was one.

When we returned to Hotel Nur, an actual Natasha—the first I'd seen—lingered a few doors down from the entrance. Her body was lean, all angles, especially the way her knees jutted out of her orange mini skirt. The only curve I could see was the curl of her bobbed platinum hair.

Chad insisted on the test. The sun made the burnt-red rooftops shimmer as I turned from him and stepped into the bathroom. His way, I figured, would produce an answer. Clarify things. I eased onto my haunches and balanced over a porcelain hole with cup in hand. Through the crack in the door, I heard the call to prayer, and afterwards, a Russian voice arguing with someone on the street below our room.

When Mary Magdalene crashed Jesus' dinner party, he recognized a fellow healer, one who could soothe with her caress. He touched her chin as she perfumed his feet with oil and turned her face up to his. "Things change," he said when they were eye to eye. "Come with me. I'll never leave you alone." The next day I would see a fresco of Mary Magdalene with regret painted in her eyes. She would appear to weep into my hair from the ceiling.

I peed, then handed Chad the stick still wet with urine.

I WISH I COULD SAY I saw Sümela's Black Madonna when I explored the monastery, but her image painted on cracked black wood and framed in eighteenth-century silver metalwork had disappeared. Maybe she resembled Our Lady of Jasna Gora: almond-shaped eyes half closed; a svelte nose lengthening her oval face; complexion the color of coffee with cream; a halo setting off the gold borders of her headpiece. Would her image have inspired me to wash my hands in her sacred spring or put the water to my lips? Perhaps I would have felt a sudden lift of spirit, a tingling from head to toe. I would have been able to step back from my life and trust everything would turn out okay.

Instead, I found stories of Black Madonnas long after my relationship with Chad was over. Two days after the hike, backpack slung over his arm, he climbed onto the airport bus. I waited for him to turn around, to change his mind. His bus roared away, the tires churning up a cloud of dust. On the outside our relationship wasn't over—and wouldn't be for another year—but on some level we'd both abandoned it.

I traveled west along the Black Sea following a route the spiritual descendants of Barnabus and Sophronius, the hermits credited with bringing Sümela's Black Madonna to Anatolia. After the monastery was founded, the two traveled throughout Anatolia, the Balkans, and Russia to sell copies of their famous icon. In Sinop I said a prayer at St. Anne's, the church of Mary's mother, whose image time had transformed into a winged, faceless figure. Alone in Safronbolu, I rambled into quiet neighborhoods where I watched women hang rugs on clotheslines and sweep stone steps. Sometimes I stood on the side of a street to watch people sauntering by, worries or hope mapped on their faces. The breeze orchestrated their voices into a medley, tuning into my heartbeat, and I dissolved into the current for a moment.

Some scholars conjecture that artists darkened Mary's image to illustrate a text from the Song of Songs: "I am black and beautiful;" others associate Black Madonnas with ancient earth goddesses; others say they express a feminine power not fully conveyed by a pale-skinned Mary and link them to Mary Magdalene. Perhaps the painter never intended her to be a "Black Madonna" and soot from centuries of burning candles turned her pigment dark. Perhaps she ended up so many miles from home by accident, a wrinkle in her predestined story. Perhaps she felt obliged to say yes. Perhaps the ways men looked at her fueled her desire to seek shelter—any shelter.

Sümela's Black Madonna never appeared to me on that hike. She was gone. Or she was everywhere. Inside the monastery, hues of paintings lightened only to be darkened again by shadows of passing clouds. Stones crumbled underfoot—the possibilities in narratives conceived. And that interior debris, what's left of desire, shifted. I wonder if Mary would choose, as I have, the stories that sustain her. I wonder if she would exist, as I have, in the spaces that they blur.

The Work of Hands

I PAUSE FROM READING A BOOK at my mother's kitchen table when she tugs the wedding ring from her left hand and places it on the window-sill. The half-moons of her fingernails mirror the nails' shiny tips, rounded and glazed with clear polish. Cracks and nicks crisscross the pads and sides of her fingers. "It's what happens when you pack boxes all day," she says, and I imagine her on the line at the clothing distribution center, her arms heaving oversized boxes onto conveyor belts, hands maneuvering them into place. I felt these hands fly through sections of my hair as she braided it every morning for years. When she begins reciting her mother's recipe for pie crust, taking flour, vinegar, shortening, and salt from the cabinets, I close the book and join her. Chocolate, coconut, and pumpkin pies will be my mother's contribution for tomorrow's Thanksgiving dinner.

As a child I never saw her assemble the ingredients. Pie shells were browned when I got up, a miniature one sprinkled with cinnamon and sugar for my brother and me. Mom woke at four every morning to work on a project that needed her undivided attention. Most often, she sewed. For me the sound of darkness is the hum of a sewing machine, the hesitation of my mother's heel poised above the pedal as she readjusts linen under the tiny silver foot. During errands to the fabric store for outfit inspiration, whenever I needed a new Easter suit, school skirt, or prom dress, I obsessed over the textures of organza, rayon, and tulle. But at home, poised to help, I couldn't imagine the pattern's geometry, the sloping curves of the cut. When I asked Mom to teach me she'd say, "Watch me like your brother does."

A snapshot memory: morning before sunrise, the wind whipping snowdrifts into piles of cotton batting. Mom bent over the machine's light, her hands pressing red fabric under the needle, one-quarter inch seam—a perfect line. My brother, in choo-choo train pajamas, stands behind her on the chair's support rod with his arms around her shoulder. He watches the muscles of her hands move from memory in ways she couldn't explain. He understood.

My medium is words, not fabrics or food. My mother slides into the real when she moves from picture to tissue paper, I jump into my imagination with the soft tap of my fingertips on the keyboard. In my first—and last—sewing project, I got as far as unfolding the pattern so it wouldn't tear, but Mom pinned the fabric in three-inch intervals as she walked around the table, sneakers squeaking on the kitchen's linoleum. By the time her sewing scissors began to slice in long, even strokes, I was bored. It looked so easy; what could I possibly learn by staring longer? Squeezing the forbidden sewing marker between my left thumb and ring finger, I practiced my signature over and over in my notebook.

I still love fabric itself. At twenty-three and living in Turkey, I collected scarves and carpets—even odd swatches I knew Mom could transform. In Urfa, a town in eastern Turkey, I spent hours writing poems in a tea garden and shopping in the covered market, a maze of stalls with the oldest parts built from stone. Turks lauded Urfa for its textiles. One visit I spotted a blue gown embroidered in gold and stopped to admire the ways its velvet shifted as I brushed it along my arm. Cut like a coat, I thought. Could I describe it to Mom if I bought material? As I left the stall with fabric in hand, a man held out a tray of pistachio baklava, beckoning me to sit down. Contrary to the sales pitch that usually followed such an invitation, we just chatted. Every once in a while he stopped to pull a pack of Marlboros out of his pressed white shirt and light one, his hand cupping the initial flame until the cigarette tip glowed.

That evening I sat in a tea garden with my journal and described a man selling a geometric-patterned carpet. As the copper sun dipped between mountain peaks, lights flickered on over the park's canopy of leaves. Women's murmuring voices drifted over from nearby tables. At intervals they laughed, which brought their hands to their faces, teal and lapis-blue sleeves shifting to reveal hennaed hands. Headscarves, tied once at the shoulders, cascaded down their backs in paisleys, rainbows, and stars. Gold bangles slid down their wrists, chiming when the women sipped tea. As I stood to leave, I saw one bend down to kiss her yawning daughter.

I WASH MY HANDS AT THE SINK before offering to help Mom make the Thanksgiving pies. A few weeks ago, I tried to make a pie with fresh pears, but I rolled out the dough three times. First my hands clenched the rolling pin handles as I fought the too-sticky dough; the disc stuck to the countertop. After cupping a handful of flour in my palms and dumping it with a sigh, I tried again. This time the dough broke apart. Finally I rolled it out and unrolled it in the pie tin without a problem. It was probably too tough to eat, but I don't know. I gave it to a friend as I'd planned—a thank-you gift for helping me out. Mom taught me that home-made gifts are the best, and I didn't have more time, extra money, or extra pears.

I've been back from Turkey for years, and I have a son, Holden. It's time to study my mother's techniques. She cuts shortening with flour, forks the mixture until blended, and rolls out a disc with a wooden pin. One time. She only skims the dough. Gentle, these hands anchored my baby's curled fingers hours after he was born.

Holden's first table food was Mom's homemade chicken and noodles; she dries the noodles overnight on the countertop. Friends and family request this dish often, and marvel how much she cooks from scratch. Even our vegetables were garden grown. Every August we canned green beans and sweet corn, and Mom could yank down corn leaves and pluck the silk faster than anyone I knew. It took me hours to snap beans; the plunk, plunk of beans falling into the container slowed as my mind drifted away from the task. I've tried to duplicate the sauce she'd make from canned tomatoes. Once I called from Turkey, waking her at midnight to ask how much oregano and basil to add. "Use your eyes," she said. "Sprinkle it in the pot until it looks good. Add more to taste."

Mom used food to establish solace in our house. During my childhood, she stayed my father's drinking with meals served right when he walked through the door. "He drank less that way," she explained. "And that's how I grew up. Mom always had dinner on the table for Dad," she said. Mom braised roast beef and baked pork chops the size of Bibles. Dad dipped the dinner rolls she made before her work—back then at my school's cafeteria—in homemade gravy. I can still hear the sizzle of steaks on the outdoor grill. In July she'd unzip peas and serve them sautéed in butter, but summer gave him more sunlight to drink by.

My hands practiced protection as well, but in a different way. One morning in Turkey, I gripped the iron bars of my school's gate and stretched out, waiting for the security guard to unlock it so I could jog around the campus perimeter as I did almost every morning. Just as my body slid into the rhythm of the run, I heard the shuffle of someone else's shoes and the snap of a twig. Along the main street to the north, shopkeepers were raising awnings and unlocking doors, fathers were walking to the bakery for breakfast bread. But I was approaching the school's south side, a wooded area. I glanced behind me. A young man approached. I stopped and turned my back to the eight-foot stone wall, expecting him to run past, but he stopped and said something.

"Anlamadım." I knew enough Turkish to say I didn't understand.

He kept talking and walking, closing the gap between us.

"Hayır." I lifted my eyebrows to emphasize the "no."

He spoke more, now with anger.

"Git," I said, interrupting. I pointed to the road. Its similar meaning English helped me remember how to say "go."

He reached out. I stepped back against the wall. As he grabbed my arm, I grasped his neck with my freehand as my kickboxing coach had taught me. My thumb landed right between a muscle in his neck and his trachea, my pinky and ring fingers curling into his neck on the other side of the tube. My strongest fingers, however, missed; instead, I sunk my nails into the shaved skin of his jaw and cheek. I pressed his gaze away and squeezed as hard as I could, yelling a friend's name into her open window across the street. No one responded, but no one needed to. He turned out of my grip and ran away.

MOM APPROACHES THE SECOND MOUND of piecrust dough. A slight swelling stiffens her fingers as she tries to wrap them around the rolling pin. Years ago, when her hands could compress fully, she made amazing birthday cakes. The night before my seventh birthday, she sifted sugar and flour and whisked egg and oil for the cake. By the time I woke up the next morning, she'd already whipped up cups of white icing, hand-dying portions robin's egg, goldenrod, and aquamarine. She squeezed hundreds of frosting stars until Holly Hobby's patched dress and calico bonnet emerged.

Eventually her hands rebelled. First it was only a tingling, and then an electric stab of nerves from her ring finger to thumb. I noticed the day she dropped a jar of olives, spheres rolling across the floor. "Carpal tunnel syndrome," she said. "Simple, outpatient surgery." I couldn't imagine the hands that upholstered davenports immobilized by bandages. When I received a Dairy Queen ice cream cake on my nineteenth birthday—even months after the surgery on her wrists—I had to hold back tears. These hands once cross-stitched enough Christmas ornaments to decorate an entire tree.

Not all the tasks of her hands have been as methodical and practiced as the way she trims or tucks the excess pie crust dough, fluting the edges with her fingertips. On a November morning in 1984, Mom found my sister, Theresa, unconscious in her garage-parked car. The coroner ruled Theresa's death accidental carbon monoxide poisoning. Mom must have slid her fingers across Theresa's neck and pressed to check for a pulse. That same hand cradled my fist as we approached Theresa's casket. Once there, our shoulders leaned into each other as we clenched hands.

In Turkey, I craved comfort food and American desserts, and while many ingredients were tough to come by, apples were plentiful. At the corner fruit stand I'd request a kilo of apples, careful not to inspect them too much and thereby offend the clerk who selected my order. Their sweet-tangy taste and crunchy texture made excellent apple crisp, apple bread, and once—an apple pie. How I rolled out the dough alone successfully is still beyond me. Perhaps the air's humidity—it had just stormed—added just enough moisture, or perhaps the marble countertops kept the dough from sticking. Maybe I even remembered my mother's advice to apply just the right amount pressure. Regardless, I took the pie over to my boyfriend's home as my contribution to dinner that evening.

As his father and stepmother reclined against the sofa, I cut and served the pie, hands shaking. I knew they'd judge my baking abilities. They praised the pie immediately after their hands brought their first bites to their lips. And twice during dessert, they burst into laughter. Proud, I asked my boyfriend to translate: "I am happy to introduce you to this American staple and a family recipe." I thought about my mother on the walk home, my homesickness interrupted by my boyfriend's occasional giggles.

"What is it?" I begged. "Just tell me. Out with it."

"My parents thought it funny," he said. "My ex-girlfriend baked them an apple pie, too."

I stopped and looked him in the eye. "What kind of Turkish woman makes apple pie?"

I could have asked: What kind of American woman can only successfully bake a pie in Turkey? Sometimes, when stakes are high, our hands remember.

MOM PICKS UP ANOTHER ROUND of dough and offers it to me: "Do you want to try?" I nod. She moves to the other side of the counter— more of a peninsula than an island—where she can watch but where her hands are less likely to interrupt. She's standing in the exact spot where I told her I'd been offered a teaching job in Turkey.

"The director gave me a couple days to think about it," I said, knowing I would accept. She stayed silent.

"They'll pay for her apartment, insurance, and taxes," Dad offered, for once on my side. "Think of how much money she'll be able to save."

"I don't want you to go, but I'll support your decision," she said eventually. I don't remember her turning out of the room because I was rubbing my palms on the back of a chair, my knuckles appearing and disappearing as they gripped the vinyl.

What I didn't know then is that my work and travel dreams inspired Mom. Several years after I moved back to the States, I dreamed up a vacation for the two of us: Italy. My responsibilities included researching the trip, preparing a shoestring budget, and handling logistics. I discovered inexpensive convents to stay in and found cheap roundtrip tickets to Rome. Two days before we left a complication arose: pregnant, I spent most of my time nauseated on the couch or vomiting in the bathroom. I didn't plan to tell her about the pregnancy so early, but I did, hoping she'd suggest we postpone or cancel our trip. She didn't.

My favorite memories of Italy are not of me slamming down my water glass next to a plate of seafood risotto and dashing to the bathroom, nor of me making a beeline from Michelangelo's *David* to the women's restroom. No, they are watching Mom finish a cross-stitch project she made as a thank-you gift for a convent, her fingertips pinching a needle as it appeared and disappeared over the horizon of stretched fabric. Sometimes after a long day touring museums and cathedrals, we sat in our room, Mom sewing and me reading, listening to church bells or the nuns' choir practice.

I often look at a photo of Mom sampling cappuccino at our favorite café in Siena. Time has been folded into the creases of her hands: dry, slightly swollen with a smattering of new liver spots. Her chin rests in one hand as she watches wedding attendees stream out onto Siena's piazza, the bride and groom smiling amid bursts of spontaneous applause. Her other hand, not in the photo, is poised next to mine. Walking arm-in-arm down the streets of Italy, we skipped pastry shops in favor of gelato. Even if Italian pastries differed from the ones we knew, the dense texture of cream and tangy fruit on our tongues delighted us. The myriad of new, intense flavors—pistachio, raspberry, lemon—enticed us back into stores almost every time we passed.

MOM STIRS IN COCONUT FLAKES for the pie filling as I pinch off excess dough from the crust I just patted down in the dish. My fluted edges are not as evenly spaced and equally pressed as hers, but I know it takes practice. She hands me the dish of dark chocolate custard to pour on top. Soon it is ready to go into the oven.

"Holden's ten months. Is he ready for cinnamon and sugar crust?"

"Absolutely," I answer, placing the extra strip of dough in a tin she offers. I prick it with a fork, brush it with butter, and sprinkle the sweet mixture on top.

She turns open her tools—her hands—and the rulers of her index fingers curve. They become shallow bowls. As a child I saw only the products of these hands—birthday cakes, skirts, and Sunday meals—not what they could teach me, even by their limitations. Now I imagine recipes written between the lines on her palm, grocery lists penciled down her fingers. The muscles of my hands contract and expand as I type, as I search for order and meaning. Always my mother's hands are there in mine.

I hand the tin of crust back to her, our fingertips touching.

Kitchen Salsa

MILLIE, MY MOTHER-IN-LAW, pours red beans into a pot to be loosened in water, softened with heat. A few legumes skitter across my countertop, the sound a maraca makes when rolled slowly. Fresh cilantro waits for my knife. Its green stems seem to stretch and bend—a dancer's arms—the leafy hands ready to flavor Dominican rice and beans far from the Caribbean in my Nebraska kitchen. In cooking, as in dance, there is rhythm: measure, stir, measure, pour. Partners, Millie and I move forward for a beat, backward for another, both returning to stillness for one beat in between.

Millie steps back from the counter. I picture her black cocktail dress shifting as she stands up from the seat in her restaurant, La Estrella del Caribe, on New Year's Eve several years ago. Our hands clutch as she pulls me to the dance floor. Her eyes laugh as her black stilettos spin. Stepping into the still present, she rests a second longer than usual against the stove, exhaustion in her sigh. Millie stirs the boiling beans, thin fingers gripping the wooden spoon, then turns to the cutting board. As she dices green peppers to sheer slips and minces onions to translucent jewels, I listen to her stories of my husband Abel's childhood and stories of her own. I imagine us cooking paella together in ten years, exchanging jokes as we crack crab legs and peel shrimp. I picture her at age ten, shoulder-to-shoulder with her older sisters, Lucy, Maria-Louisa, and Lydia, cooking for their family of ten-turning-twenty. In my kitchen she rinses rice and swishes water in the bowl with a flick of her wrist. Her diamond and sapphire ring glints under the water. Someday, she'll pull my son, Holden, close to her on a dance floor, his child-arm touching her waist as she guides his feet.

Millie shifts her weight with her knees to create a hip sway just as she does on the dance floor. Her spine lengthens, straightens, and just like a dancer, she switches directions as I follow her lead—add a dollop of tomato paste and tablespoon of olive oil to the beans. I raise an eyebrow when Millie abruptly breaks to rest on the couch, but I don't consider tumors.

One step forward moves us eighteen months from my kitchen to her laundry room the last time we will speak in person. She will summon the energy to fold her son's t-shirts, her bony hands smoothing out the wrinkles in white cotton.

"I'm so afraid for you to die," I'll say, breaking down.

"It'll be fine," she'll reply, turning to face me.

"I love you so much," I'll say.

We'll embrace. I'll sway a bit as I do when I'm anxious.

In salsa, an experienced dancer improvises by turning a single spin into a double or triple, even without her partner's set up. But I'm left with a 4 x 6-inch index card, "small red onion," "half a green pepper" scrawled on the lines in my handwriting.

I waited almost a year before making rice and beans.

"How do you know if there's enough sauce?" I ask Abel. He slips one hand around my waist and scoops up some beans with a wooden spoon.

"I don't know exactly," he says, "but these taste good."

"Great. Time for the cilantro," I say, handing Holden a fragrant cup. I pick him up and he dumps the cilantro into the pot. I shift my knees and turn, putting Holden on my hip. Abel opens the top of another pan.

"Con-con," he says, pushing a wooden spoon into the grains until he reaches a crisp layer of rice at the bottom. He steps back and for a moment I imagine him as a child sneaking some from his mother's pot. When he shifts back the three of us stand before the simmering meal; Abel leans forward to kiss me, his long, graceful fingers squeezing my hand.

Toward Defining Intimate Space

AFFECTION

"Now be still. I've got lipstick," I say. My grandfather reclines in his La-Z-Boy and stares beyond me at the television. I position my hand near his jaw and his breath, which smells like Carnation condensed milk and coffee, warms my fingers. As I reach over for a tissue to blot, he speaks.

"A chicken bit my chin right here," he points to his dimple. "Took a whole chunk off."

"Bull," I reply, tempted to add the second half of the word he'd planted into my vocabulary. Really, I believe him.

I blend rouge into his stubbled cheeks and change the subject. "We have the same blue eyes." I squint to inspect my work. We both know that isn't true; he's my dad's stepfather.

His silver-streaked black hair rolls up easily in Grandma's pink plastic curlers because he only washes it once a week. I brush dandruff from his shoulders, smelling his age and sweat and body oils. Then I hold up a mirror: "Ta da!" He pretends to be startled, then smiles.

As I'm cleaning up, Grandpa reaches into his pocket for a cigarette. Lighting the Pall Mall, he barks, "Chrissy, get me a beer." In the ten steps from refrigerator to chair, I shake the Pabst Blue Ribbon. He acts surprised by the burst as he cracks it open even though it's our ritual. Makeover misted, we laugh as rivulets of beer spill over the side of the can. Minutes pass as we share the quiet space, the television show's laugh track anchoring our thoughts.

DEEP UNDERSTANDING

Johan and I spoon in his sleeping bag on the open deck of a ferry from Santorini to Athens. I'd been shaking sand off my sandals when we made eye contact on Samos five days ago. After he opened a guidebook, I struck up a conversation. We walked into town, rented a scooter, and spent an afternoon admiring the markets, stucco houses, and whitewashed churches.

"I've never seen this," I'd said at one point, slipping off the scooter. "The way groves of trees end at small cliffs…"

"Above a turquoise sea." He finished my sentence. Shoulder to shoulder, we listened to wind shaking leaves. That night, while munching on gyros, we braided our travel itineraries.

This ferry trip marks our last few hours together. We're already sorting our memories.

"Weren't those charcoal grains of sand on Santorini amazing?" I ask. We had sipped cocktails on a black-sand beach discussing the island's ancient ruins, the Minoan-Crete civilization, and the lost city of Atlantis.

"Volcanic residue the texture of table salt." Johan's hand moves across my arm to zip up the sleeping bag.

"From the mountain the beaches looked like roads."

The sand in Ios, where we'd been just three days before, was the size of mustard seeds. There, I placed the pink, yellow, and white grains on my fingertip for Johan to study. He brought my hand up to eye level and turned his head. "Translucent," he said. From a few steps away it must've looked as if we were about to kiss. I opened my fingers, let the sand slide through, and asked about South African beaches. In a bar on the "Home of Homer," where we tried to channel the Bard and conversed for hours.

"Can you quote any lines?" he challenged me, an English teacher.

"Two friends, two bodies, with one soul inspired," I mustered. Johan smiled, hand wrapped around a cold beer.

"I bet Homer preferred wine: 'Wine gives strength to weary men,'" he paused. "You tended bar once?"

"I enjoyed mixing liquor and word play," I said. "Especially sexual innuendo drinks: Buttery Nipple, Between the Sheets, Sex on the Beach." The night ended dancing on the bar-turned-disco.

When the cold breeze picks up across the water, Johan and I cleave to each other. This is the closest our bodies have been. Tomorrow we will part at the bus station without a kiss, but now, as he pulls me close, I can feel the grains of sand, released from the folds of the bag, on his skin. We whisper on into the night, anticipating each other's every word.

PRIVATE

Aurora, Prairie, Airline, Meredith. At eight years old, I wrote the names of my neighborhood's streets on curling birch bark with a felt-tip pen. I admired the letters' shapes: I resembled a tree—slim yet solid and as a vowel quite generative, an anchor for consonants; M: became tree trunks in a forest; the uppercase Y reached like branches; capital A looked like the spade I used to dig a hole near the birch where I buried my scrolls after rolling and binding them with string.

When I planted my words, I imagined another girl—a sister in love with language—would find them and speak them aloud. The a's in Aurora would pin down the purr-like roar. She'd conjure the grass-waves with the last syllable of Prairie, and she'd marry the logical precision of geometry with the balloon-filled promise in Airline. And Meredith: a name of substance with a strange and splendid drop; would my imagined sister think the word felt as gritty and rich in her mouth as it did in mine— so much like the soil in which we dug?

A sliver of me existed in the geography of roads running east and west and in the fruit of these words' meanings. From the Aurora I knew as a child—the princess of *Sleeping Beauty*—leapt the northern lights, the Roman goddess of dawn, an asteroid. Prairie conjured more than the title of Laura Ingalls Wilder books; it built the horizon of my birth, a landscape to which I'd return. Airline suggested an escape route, a way to move from the imagination to the real. And Meredith—no one I knew yet—became a character who serves an old queen, an entrepreneur who speaks French and Japanese, a paleontologist who discovers a new species of dinosaur.

I don't remember if it was before or after the planting of words that I dusted off my mother's high school Spanish book to teach myself a new language, nor do I recall the year I read the A encyclopedia cover to cover. Did these words sprout after I read the eight-hundred paged *World's Best Fairy Tales*? Chronology's importance evaporates when the smell of words—dirt and dusty paper—rise from concrete streets after a summer rain.

SEXUAL

With the water of the hot tub so warm, I don't know where I begin. Rain blurs the order of things, conversations dissolve. I pour expensive beer for the box seat holders at the Des Moines Grand Prix and notice Ryan. Behind him, storm clouds gather and a few drops fall. The temp agency doesn't call when the rivers are rising. We have a conspicuous amount of time. When we need to eat, we talk over lobster bisque, salmon sautéed in butter. Once, after he drops me off at home, we talk all night on the phone; it rains five inches on both sides of town. Once, an Irish wolfhound meets me at the door of his dad's house. I shake water off my feet. We watch *Casablanca* while a sluice cascades down windows. Rain bounces up from the deck of his lush backyard. Puddles grow into pools. Lightening pulls us into blankets of steam. I feel thunder's vibrations ripple out from the small of my back.

COMFORT

"In what dress did you feel the most beautiful?" I ask the empty bedroom as I lift out cherry-red silk and black taffeta gowns off the rack. Images of my mother-in-law, Millie, wearing them materialize before shifting to stills of a yesterday's events: the hospice nurse closing Millie's eyes, death returning color to her face.

I ooh and ahh at each dress as I'm sure Millie did, caressing the fabric and inspecting for rips or stains. "I've only seen you dressed in white in your wedding photos," I say, admiring a sequined dress. I can almost hear her laughing; the price tag, still attached, reveals a bargain. I'm five inches taller than Millie and a size eight on a good day, so when sizes zero, two, four, and six give way to a purple strapless in size ten, I try it on. I wiggle out of my yoga pants, slipping the satin over my head. Rosettes line the curved bodice. The dress swishes around my ankles.

Millie and I "shopped" together for the first time in this room shortly after her son and I married. Opening a chest of clothes, she asked: "Would any of these jeans fit you?" For an hour I pulled on and peeled off jeans as we chatted. Every so often, she'd snag a blouse or sweater from her closet: "This would look good with that pair." I felt closest to Millie when we shared a vocabulary of texture, color, and shape.

I turn to her purse rack. A black Prada tumbles off when I remove a brown crocodile skin handbag. I open it, hoping to find a lipstick, fingernail file, or sales receipt. Nothing—no lint, stray pen marks, or forgotten pennies—not even in the black-beaded clutch. Under the rack I find a cloth bag containing four Fendi purses, the same style in black, chocolate brown, tan, and red. All pristine. My fingers crawl through drawers of scarves: wine-colored rayon, Indian silk with elephants, ochre and gold floral, variations of blue geometric designs. I sigh, wrapping two of them around my shoulders. I cocoon in memories and miss her.

FAMILIAR

Cars no longer rush by on Vine Street at two o'clock in the morning. No one stomps across the room in the apartment upstairs. In our world, my son and I are the only people awake. Lamplight falls across the bed, the glow throwing geometric shadows on the wall and elongating the lines of his crib. As I cradle his head in my arm and feel his warmth, we share the space of my body—his lip-lock around my nipple, the milk moving between us.

At only thirty-hours old he summoned me. And now I'm stirred from the deepest dream by his sigh, his cries, his urgent hunger. With my breasts thick with milk, I apply my new language: sleep bra, nursing tee, football clutch, cross-cradle, express milk. In a few months he will knead my breasts with tiny fists as if they are loaves of dough, jerking his head back to coax a faster flow.

He calls up love from the marrow of my bones.

I doze. The blanket thrown over the tall-backed rocking chair makes a soft thud each time we tip back. He drifts off: suck, suck, pause; suck, suck, pause. I move him to my shoulder, pat him, and whisper in his ear, planting secrets he may recognize in the distant chapters of his life. Before I place him in the crib, I kiss his forehead; his breath smells yeasty and sweet. It flutters like rice paper, making the sound of "H."

New Lens

PRESENCE

After his international flight touched down in Krakow, Poland, after he refused buttered bread despite obvious hunger, after he stripped down to big-boy underwear white and tight around his waist, my three-and-a-half-year-old son, Holden, flies from feather pillow to feather pillow. He lifts his tangerine-colored cast, arm broken on a playground the week before, and puffs out his chest. 10:30 p.m. He kicks his wrinkled pajamas back into the suitcase. "I don't want to go to bed!"

He exhausts himself to a heap of giggles on the floor. I try to gather him up. His neck arcs back toward the window, and he tries to turn out of my arms. My hold tightens despite his sobs. "You'll feel so much better after sleeping," I say. With one finger, I stroke his hair until his cries soften. I sing "Twinkle, Twinkle, Little Star" until his wings surrender.

EXPERIENTIAL

My family is a gaggle of geese burdened with backpacks, luggage rolling behind us like waddling goslings, rain sliding off our slick umbrellas. An hour past Holden's bedtime, we find the right platform, proper train, assigned car, correct couchette. I anticipate Holden squawking at the bunk's tight fit—I insist we share—but our bodies spoon in a nest of sweatshirts and blankets.

The odor of worn vinyl polished with skin-oils and grime and the smelly size thirteens of the snoozing Czech on the bottom bed don't distract Holden.

"A train, a train, we'll sleep on a train," he says. I recall his toy trains, the wooden tracks.

"Do you hear the engines?" I ask. He nods. "Now listen for the whistle," I whisper in his ear. The train pulls out of the station. "Remember this," I say aloud. To whom am I really speaking? I want to remember Holden unfolding during this two-week trip to Krakow, Prague, and Munich; remember his confident skip across a park in Krakow holding his Uncle T.J.'s hand; remember him nibbling a dumpling and laughing as he shares a bowl of pierogis with his Grandma Sharon; remember the five of us on a horse-drawn carriage ride, Holden snug and rapt between Abel and me—mom, child, dad.

We rock as the train rolls through the Polish countryside, and I wait for the swaying to lull him to sleep. He lies still but awake for almost an hour. The breeze from the open window kisses his hair.

ABSENCE

We don't take Holden to Auschwitz-Birkenau. I can't explain the piles of children's shoes: red crisscross topped, Dutch clogs, galoshes; the piles of woven baskets and black suitcases, names and numbers written in white; the piles of hair and textiles made from it. Shafts of light show where Nazis dropped Zyklon B. My preschooler doesn't need to see me weep, without words, as I imagined mother after mother after mother hugging their terrified children in the seconds before death. For "efficiency." The numbers. Experiments on tender bodies. Using ash, fat, bones. Of children. For things. Behind the fence I see a cottage, imagine a garden—lilies and lilacs, early lettuce and herbs—and the blond-haired children of the commander romping around in the dirt and wearing the clothes of the dead.

COLLAPSE OF IMAGINATION AND REALITY

Holden play-acts for the first time. I watch as if he's on stage. Shiny marble reflects his silhouette and the dark-chocolate irises of his eyes flicker against the whiteness of the rest. Shoulders flush against the wall, Holden turns his head so he can listen for pirates clanking down the halls of the Hotel Polonia in their sailor boots. "Shhhh... they're following me," he says. After fire-breathing dragon statues, after castles with knights in armor, after caves with crystals sparkling on the insides, after hearing conversations he can't unpuzzle, anything is possible. Holden becomes one of Them. He spies the skull and crossbones flag and now he claims the treasure chest near the elevator with the heel of his sandal. Are there more secrets hidden about the first floor's tables and chairs? In Holden's storybooks, his shadow could peel itself off the wall and help search for gold and jewels. For now, he pauses in thought, his full lips pursed, and he thinks the shadows alive.

PUZZLE

We follow a map's serpentine sidewalks and labyrinthine streets. Right angles morph into loops, curves. Splashes of green, blue, and gray mirror the grassy park, the painted buildings, the steel-colored cloud cover. There's a faceless human form, down on elbows and knees, plopped near a playground with a giant skull on its back. The guidebook's clues: *Parable of a Skull* (1993) by Jaroslav Rona.

Holden's response: on tiptoe, he circles the bronze sculpture without placing his hand inside the empty eye socket or sliding his hand down the smooth, cold thigh; how his silence pulls me back into myself—robs me of exact words. The vocabulary of art I know suddenly condensed into the map's key, two-dimensional and dated, directions turned around. Holden turns to me and solves the moment with his own question, his own answer: "Why is he crawling? Babies crawl."

MIRRORS

For a moment, Uncle T.J. and Holden regard each other through a system of lenses: T.J.'s vintage Super Eight and a sharper, digital machine. The video camera wobbles, but Holden holds it carefully, understanding the gravity of this outlawed toy. "Look through this part," T.J. says, pointing to the concave well. Holden turns, pressing his eye into the viewfinder. "You can change what you see," T.J. says. "Fuzzy, far away, close up."

Someday, Holden may want to skew his view of the world, warp the beauty, find the angle of light in an otherwise dark and somber shot. Someday, Holden may wish to manipulate the focus, scope. Now, new frames shape his point of view. Perhaps not Culture or History. Not Language or Geography. Snapshots and ten-second videos: zigzagging through trails in vineyards; scaling hundreds of castle steps; Introduction to Checkers with T.J. in a hotel lobby; the hornless rhino at the Munich Zoo; foil-covered chocolates in the shapes of ladybugs and beetles placed on hotel pillows. And I observe closely because we're not in our kitchen making dinner, not walking down Main Avenue in our town of 20,000, but in Europe, undistracted by work and phone calls and the buzz of regular life. We're zooming on a train toward the Bavarian Film Studios—the Super Eight in Holden's hands pointed at the suburbs of Munich stretching alongside—as T.J. snaps photo after photo after photo.

INDEPENDENCE

The goat with white and gray-brown spots butts into throngs of kids, sniffs strollers, nudges parents' purses and pockets. It mesmerizes Holden as much as the shiny golden dog decorating a sculpture on the St. Charles Bridge in Prague did.

Holden sees fists opening, fingers flat, and the goat grinding the pebbles of food. Does he imagine crawling on its back, digging his heels in, riding away? He wants to feed the bullet-sized pebbles to the goat by *himself*. He slides a coin into the machine, hears the *clink, clink* as he cranks the dispenser knob.

Just as Holden opens the metal door, the goat shoves his shoulders into Holden's thigh and slaps his front hooves on the food dispenser, mouth under the door. Not a flicker of hurt or disappointment crosses Holden's face, but he gets closer, his hand against the goat's stringy coat.

The image of Pan—god of fields, groves, and glens—flickers in my mind. And I remember that Holden means "from a hollow in the valley." I picture Holden-as-Pan—grown up, of course—roaming the forest with nymphs and cracking them up with his ornery jokes. His pipe-playing rivals the birds' spring melodies.

SPONTANEITY

We're exhausted from sightseeing in Krakow and it has started to rain. We slip into a café for tea and choose decadence: dessert for dinner.

My mother orders Polish Apple Pie, *szarlotka*, the tender slices of apple just as juicy as an American would wish, yet it surprises with a buttery crust, slightly sweeter than her own recipe. T.J. orders tiramisu, each layer of Mascarpone, ladyfingers, and creamy cocoa with a hint of liqueur adding a new level of flavor. The décor of flapper photos and 1920s furniture makes me feel golden, bubbly, as if I should order champagne, but instead Abel and I order Dark Chocolate Cake, bitterness countered with a bit of sugar and creamy butter. It blossoms in my mouth. For Holden, we choose something substantial—crepes, the thin, delicate disks served with thick, hot orange sauce. Vitamin C at least.

Coffee is ordered all-around. Except Holden. He orders "hot chocolate"—a request taken literally. The waiter serves melted chocolate layered with cream and steamed milk. Sometimes delight arrives in the simple bend of a rule. We stir the layers and Holden eats it with a spoon.

BEAUTY

For Holden, Prague in spring won't be pastel buildings of ornate frosting trim—Easter eggs under a dark carton of rain clouds—but following white peacocks through a hedge-maze at the Wallenstein Gardens. He meanders with the bushes' turns, ignores the rough branches scratching his legs. As he pushes through a dead-end, Holden gets close. When he digs into his pockets for the last piece of biscuit, the bird approaches, chest puffed. He turns his crowned head, looking at the boy's offered morsel. For a second their eyes lock. Then trust appears, and his beak lunges forward. Snap. An empty hand. I fear the danger of sharp beak and child skin, and yet the fan of white eyes consumes me. I want to stroke a feather with my fingertip, pluck it, hold it against me so it may never change even as its colors shift, pearlescent, in the light. Holden stares at the bird in awe. May he always trust that beauty waits if he risks the reach.

Beyond Sound

A STACCATO DOWNBEAT—the hand-drum's thump—kept time as the sax player's fingers plucked a dizzy harmony full of quick turns. Sound skipped on my skin. The clarinet's lilting melody whirled past our table as my colleagues and I nibbled typical Turkish dessert: melons, berries, oranges. Stay for coffee, conversation, dancing, the music teased. But we paid our bill, said *güle güle*, and walked across the boulevard near Istanbul's Blue Mosque. The sun had pulled its veil across the Sultanahmet neighborhood and winter's darkness eclipsed the baths and bazaars.

It may have been my full belly of lamb kabob, sautéed eggplant, lentil soup, and pita, but more likely it was the heightened awareness I had developed living in a foreign place that compelled me to receive and catalog more consciously the sounds of my new environment: catcalls from Marlboro-smoking men on the corner, screeches of mini-buses, the new blends of consonants and vowels strung along the necklace of speech.

This meta-layer, this readiness to hear, made the night feel sensuous. Windows seemed like transparent skin; the let-down drapes swept across like a woman's hair. Streets yawned empty. I could almost hear the *swish swish* of Istanbulites inside their homes where fathers kissed their infants goodnight, where old women walked barefoot across wooden floors, where newlyweds brushed shoulders. Then the mosque's lights switched on. I paused, imagining the muezzin raising his eyes for the first lines of the *adhan*.

The invitation to hear more deeply may arrive in an envelope of sound. It comes in clean paper, its white edges crisp. No stamp, no return address. A mystery. As I slide my fingernails under the open corner, a sample of noise—a humming refrigerator, a popping heater, a honking car—erases expectations. Then, a swelling of stillness. And this prepares me to listen.

I had heard the Call to Prayer before. Two hours into my first deep sleep since my plane touched down in Istanbul, Allah's name trumpeted me awake. Every day for two years, the Call urged me out of bed. It invited me to slip on sweatpants and sandals and walk down the street to buy fresh bread. In Tarsus, the muezzins sang off-key, but five times a day their chanting pulled me out of the currents of teaching, cooking, and reading for a moment of centering.

This night, however, I heard the Call standing right outside the mosque. The sound system crackled. There was a slight pause before a singular, unadorned baritone burst forth: Al—LAHHHHHHHHHH. The first syllable, Al, clipped like a pole-vaulter's jump. The LAHHHH-HHH the soar through the air—clear, tuned, persuasive.

The sound cleaved to me. Two syllables stripped away the barriers of language and custom and history that made me an outsider. The black sky and its array of stars remained. My body's edges seemed to loosen as if part of me wanted to move with the sound. I caught my breath. When sound ushers me into realization, I feel called not to belief, but to connection.

THE DAY FOLLOWING A THIRTY-HOUR LABOR that ended in C-section, I listened to a Nebraska blizzard batter St. Elizabeth's Hospital. Wind whistled across the parking lot and slammed into windows. Even though bright fluorescent lights and the glow of televisions remind-ed me of the presence of other patients, I felt singular. I was adrift in the fuzz of sleep deprivation and the blur of hormone overload when I heard Holden's alarm-clock cry, the wail of a newborn confused by light, air, hunger. His lungs measured his breathy siren out at regular intervals, as if an accordion's bellows playing the same note over and over: waaaaah (breath) waaaaah (breath) waaaaah (breath).

In this room of plastic cabinets and metal furniture, sound travels best. That sound moves best through matter is odd to me because sound appears invisible; like wind, I can only see its interactions with other things: the tips of spruce, an American flag, a woman's winter scarf. But the denser the matter—a bed or a building or a body—the closer the molecules exist; with particles bonded together, sound is transferred almost immediately from one to the next. The eardrums actually *feel* a sound's vibration, so sound only *seems* intangible.

When Holden cried that night, my body responded to a visceral, unnamable truth that altered my consciousness. With his cry, my milk let down. Thin liquid streamed from my tingling nipples. My heart quickened. Urgency overwhelmed me not because my body was working in new ways or because my soaked, cotton gown embarrassed me or because I was shocked by Holden's urgency but because clear tubes (post-surgery fluids) strapped me to the bed. I couldn't get to him.

In the two or three minutes it took for the nurse to arrive, loosen his swaddling, and hand him to me, his cry remade a familiar world—with me at its center—into another. When Holden latched onto my nipple and I heard the *shoost shoost* of milk, the room's white walls, hard-edged rectangles, and steel bed blurred. In that space just beyond my skin, Holden and I were anchored. Connected. Evolution over millennia developed the call and response of chemical reactions, but at the time, I couldn't put words to the symphony of hormones. I couldn't make meaning yet. Skin to skin, we waited for the snow to cease and for the wind to slow. Then we slept.

AFTER I TOURED THE ATOMIC BOMB MUSEUM in Hiroshima, Japan with its staggering statistics and stark depictions of horror, after I visited the Memorial Mound with its thousands of unclaimed, cremated dead, after I walked past the river and its ghosts of burning corpses, after I listened to groups of somber children queued up singing songs in the park, I stood before the Peace Bell. The dome-shaped belfry represents the world, its metal skin a map with no national boundaries.

When sound invites me to hear deeply, sometimes I name this moment immediately, as if the sound breaks up into letters and floats into my consciousness. Other times it takes years to do so, the moment's meaning elusive. Some invitations open only when my brain, by understanding context and history, gives them weight.

I raised the clapper, whispered my intention for a peaceful world, and let go. The clapper contacted the bell. A note near to the lowest piano key emanated. Just below it, a sound like static, a hum under the deep bass tone. In my ear, the vibrations from the single, rich note moved through the hammer, anvil, and stapes to the snail-shaped cochlea where cells absorbed it. So close to the bell, I felt the rippling waves push against and through my skin. Paradox: how this deep, physical hearing urged connection with the world beyond me.

When auditory nerve fibers picked up the triggered electrical signals and carried them to my brain, I named the sound. Knowledge gave significance to that name. And so the bell's sound could no longer be just sound because now this sound carried the flash of light, fire on the skin, crumbled buildings and beings, leukemia, genes corrupted for generations.

The waves rippled beyond me. I was present to the sound and the sound released me into silence.

I CULTIVATE THESE SOUND INVITATIONS by accepting opportunities to travel or to stand on new ground. Still, I wonder how many I've missed. Too often I shroud myself in expectations. Distractions can stop up my ears like cotton swabs. Poignant moments rise from memory, a silent montage of missed sounds. At Auschwitz, I wore headphones to hear the tour guide's commentary of the concentration camp; I didn't know that Kate, my student who had taken me by the arm, was crying until I saw her tears. In Siena, Italy the maze of cobbled streets dizzied me; perhaps I missed the bells ringing out as a wedding party burst forth from the church into the piazza. I watched wind carrying clouds over the green pastures of Ireland, but I don't recall the sound of the ever-present rain. I remember Holden's first laugh—a cascade of giggles as we were playing "catch" with his squishy ball—but not the moment he said his first word. In his baby book, I inscribed "Mama, Da, ball," but I have no memory of where or when he uttered those words.

Perhaps I've missed hundreds of opportunities to lose the feeling of self for a moment and connect with another person, another pursuit, another phenomenon. Without sound, a layer is lost, a dimension absent. Without sound, there are no vibrations on my skin, nothing activating the bones in my ear. I can only wonder about how sound would've opened up the experience.

THE TRAIN RESTING ON THE PLATFORM in Stryszów, a village in southern Poland, sounded like a sigh. Perhaps it was my exhale, the auditory mix of exhaustion and the relief of arrival. The air smelled warm, moist, as if fog could materialize at any moment. Our hosts met our small contingent of students and professors at the station and stowed our bags in their cars, but we chose to walk through the village.

I noticed the subtle sounds of life as we passed the empty, two-room station. A brown chicken pecked its way around the yard. Colors buzzed:

homes and stores crackled tangerine, buttercup, ochre, and lime; blossoms rang out in crimson, cornflower blue, violet. The bright green of grass, trees, and shrubs became the melody of spring. Even the children who attended classes in the long, white school chimed in with their butterfly and flower cutouts taped to windows. As I trekked up the narrow, steep fork of the main road, I felt the turn to storm: bright colors to a gray palette of sky, warm air to cool breeze, the smell of dusty air to the smell of rain. At the hilltop church, sound intensified, the priest's chants and congregation's response broadcast from inside. With distinct syllables muffled by the audio system, I couldn't understand if they used Latin or Polish, but I recognized the rhythms of the prayers. The priest began by landing on a note and holding it—the sound of an open hand—a note into which he inserted a secession of clipped consonants. The congregation repeated the refrain.

This time, however, the chanting converged with another sound, and the envelope—the invitation—arrived. It pushed me further into the moment, crystallizing that second of time. The deep bass rumble of thunder rolled across the sky, across the mountains blurred by distant rain, across the clusters of trees, across the thin slices of pasture, across the cemetery tombs. The tympani of thunder collided; I heard a crack of lightning right above my head. This crash of sounds fused memories of prayer with sounds of the storm, layering old memories with a new one: the image of charcoal-colored clouds stampeding toward me like a heard of bison, the air chilling my skin as it pushed past me like a flood of ghosts.

The moment before it began to rain, before our clothes became stuck to our skin, before we began to run down the gravel road, before we began to shriek in delight, I felt my body's membranes give a little. I felt lighter, looser, as if walking out to the first thaw of snow after five long winter months. And then the clouds opened.

BEYOND SOUND WEAVES MOSQUE, milk, sky, stars, the touch of the living and the touch of the dead.

Beyond sound fuses vibration and reflection and paper.

"Mama, I love the movie theatre of my life," Holden, now a kindergartener, says. He scoops up a fork full of spaghetti, sauce dripping onto the side of green beans. And he hums, a robust hum, somewhere between "yum, yum, yum" and a chant. I tease out this sound, holding it in my ear. As I breathe his song into my body, I jot down his words and the tenor of his sound.

Filaments of Prayer

Anything large enough for a wish to light upon is large enough to hang a prayer upon.
—George MacDonald

The function of prayer is not to influence God, but rather to change the nature of the one who prays.

—Soren Kierkegaard

"PLEASE, GOD," I SOB, THROWING MYSELF ON MY BED. "Not this. I can't lose this baby."

I'm ten weeks pregnant and I've found a spot of dried blood on my underwear. Nothing materialized on toilet paper, but I ran to grab *What to Expect When You're Expecting* off the bookshelf. A lot of blood and pain "stronger than menstrual cramps" might mean impending miscarriage. How does one quantify blood? Each twinge in my abdomen becomes a cramp, and each cramp pushes a wave of panic rippling through my body.

I fold my hands together and plead: "Not this pregnancy. Please. Maybe another but not my first."

THE DOZEN WOMEN I OBSERVED KNEELING at the tomb of Salim Chisti of Sikri—an Indian sheikh whom the king had honored for prophesying an heir, a son—opened their palms to catch blessings from heaven. Light through the white marble latticework enclosing the tomb created intricate shadows on the walkway where I stood. From a few meters' distance, red veins shimmered through the latticework's entwined circles.

"WHAT DO YOU THINK?" I ask my husband, Abel.

"It doesn't seem like you should worry unless more blood comes." He reaches out to me with one arm and cradles a box of tissues in the other. Leaning into him, I cry. I whisk the tissues out one by one. "Please, please, please," I whisper.

"It'll be okay," Abel says. "Call the nurse. You'll feel better."

I nod. I blow my nose and take a deep breath. I check to see if the spot has grown. It has not. Still, I imagine the growing baby drowning.

I find my midwife's number. The rings sound like jingle bells except clipped—one shake, then nothing—until a faraway voice: "Please leave a message."

WHEN I STEPPED CLOSER to the Sheikh's tomb, the circles melted into an etched web. The veins were braided threads tied onto the marble. The women's chanted prayers compelled me to search my belongings for something to add. I forget what I prayed for as I laced a red thread through the curves of cool marble, but I remember a peaceful sensation as I slipped into the sacred space and listened for what surfaced.

I PACE BACK AND FORTH in our apartment until the midwife's nurse calls me back.

"How much blood?" she asks. "What color is it?"

"Dark," I reply, "As if it has been there for hours."

"Then relax. It sounds normal. Most women bleed a bit during their first trimester."

I don't see more blood the next morning and sigh, "Thank God." After a few weeks, when I see my son bouncing around via ultrasound, I decide my prayer has been answered.

A year after he is born, I read that childless women pray for sons at the tomb of Salim Chisti. I recall kneeling before the latticework, tying a double knot, and opening my hands.

❧

"HI. IT'S ME," I WHISPER, gripping my car's steering wheel with one hand, my belly with the other. "Are you there? Are you staying? Are you leaving?" Without knowing how, I know this blood differs from the spotting I experienced with my first pregnancy three years before.

Twenty minutes ago, Rosie, the physician's assistant at the Urgent

Care Clinic, told me the urine sample tested positive for pregnancy. But I bled ten days ago and now I'm bleeding again, my uterus a soaked, wrung-out rag. Rosie said I may not be miscarrying, to get blood work in two days. If hormone levels have increased or decreased, I'll know. Although I have been trying to conceive for months, I could feel the threads of hope and fear twist along my spine. Fear roots me; hope keeps me standing.

NEAR THE FISHING VILLAGE of Narlıkuyu in Turkey, I'd been suspended, hovering between Heaven— a wide sinkhole navigated by a long series of steps—and Hell, a narrow, stalactite-studded cave accessible via a shaft on a steel ladder. Between Heaven and Hell, hundreds of people had wound tourniquets around the slender wrists of a Wish Tree. For centuries visitors had secured their wishes to this and other trees like it scattered across Anatolia—the collective desire to make prayer visible. The chirps of birds bounced off the rock walls of Heaven as tourists attached prayers to the Wish Tree before moving off to explore the church ruins.

"IF YOU'RE THERE," I CONTINUE, rubbing my skin over my sweat-soaked t-shirt. "If you're staying, then I welcome you with open arms. You're wanted and loved by your parents."

Rosie, who had said not to worry because she bled with all her pregnancies, had tried to comfort me. "I never miscarried. Maybe you won't either."

"If you aren't there," I say, imagining a tiny speck within me, "if you've left already, I'm sorry I didn't get a chance to know you. Know there will be another chance for you, and that I'll be okay." I've tossed a spool of thread into an abyss and I wait for the tug of the landing. Yet I can't help but wonder: Will I know when this prayer is answered? Why do I expect that it will be, that I'll feel the recoil of the thread?

WITH THE PIT OF HEAVEN—250 meters long, 110 meters wide, and 60 meters deep—opened behind me, I clutched the tissue and composed my prayer. If the wind had picked up, the tissue might have blown down to the musty fifth-century church and flown through one of the window arches of the wall still standing, or it might have sailed over to the bushes growing between cracks and on ledges in the otherwise sheer face of rock. *Please keep my heart from breaking*, I whispered. As I tied the twisted rope on a split branch reaching east and west, I imagined the people who had built the chapel's foundations, those who had wiggled down through a crack in the earth just a few meters away and, despite their expectations, experienced Hell's dark beauty.

I ARRIVE HOME. For the rest of the day, I play with my two-year old son at a community carnival. I excuse myself frequently to check the maxi pad for clots, just as Rosie instructed. The bleeding stops for two days. But on the third blood fills pad after pad and I look for what the red heat of my body has sloughed. A nurse calls me about the blood work. I don't need her to explain the decreased numbers of my hormone count. And she doesn't offer.

AT THE WISH TREE I eclipsed the possibility of a leaf with worries of new romance. Bunches of leaves unfurled between wishes and branch-ends, a fertility unasked for but bestowed. I ascended the stairs to Heaven's edge and turned my back to the mouth of Hell. Two hundred plus twisted and tied pieces of gauze on the Wish Tree transformed slate-colored branches into striped, white arms lifted skyward. In the breeze, strips of white cotton shirts and sections of linen fluttered on the branches like butterflies.

～

"DON'T REMEMBER ANY OF THIS. Never write about this," I say aloud when I slide down my underwear and see bright red stains. I try to turn off the part of my mind that catalogs details. Sobbing, I squeeze shut my eyes. "It's happening again, again."

Abel, who is feeding our son breakfast, knocks on the bathroom door.

"What's wrong?"

"I'm bleeding. I'm losing one again."

"What do you want me to do?"

"Call in sick."

He does and takes our son to daycare.

An hour later I write in my journal: *All I want is to be taken care of, for someone to lift this feeling from me like it's a blanket, unwrap the grief that cocoons me.*

A WHITE-TURBANED PRIEST had approached me on the streets of Pushkar, India, to lead me to prayer. The guidebook warned of Brahmins who hound tourists until they pay for blessings, but I followed willingly, pulled by the idea of moving through another's ritual. I wanted to draw down assurances from all possible gods. The buildings bleached whiter as the path narrowed, and the air, scented with wood and dung from morning cooking fires, became saturated with stale water. At the end of the dirt path, I saw an expanse of marble. Women in saris the colors of mango flesh and lime rinds stood in scattered pairs around the perimeter of steps that end in a large, rectangular pool.

FOR THE ONE WEEK I'VE KNOWN I was pregnant, I have tried to will the filaments of my own flesh. Each morning I said, "This one will be fine." Every hour I placed my hand over my belly button and whispered, "Grow healthy, grow strong, grow whole." I have taken a pregnancy test every other day to see the magenta line darken. I kept it a secret for five days so I could tell Abel on his birthday. The silly card had a picture of a cat and words about sweet birthday surprises. The gift contained a bag of Kit Kats—his favorite—and a frame with the pregnancy test strip taped inside. Underneath, the words: "See you this spring, Daddy. Love, Your Second due March 21."

PIGEON DROPPINGS COVERED THE STEPS leading to the water, but I kicked off my sandals when the priest removed his shoes, tiptoeing down to the water where we squatted together. He sprinkled drops of water on my head, and he showered me in Hindi prayers. I breathed it all in—the words I knew—Shiva, Krishna, Brahma—and those I didn't. I gave him my hands, palms up. He took them in his before dipping my fingertips into the water. "We pray for your family now," he said in English. "Your parents? Your brothers? Sisters? Children? Name them." I did, a litany of living and dead and mere possibilities.

I KNOW THERE'S NOTHING I can do to stop the bleeding, so I shut the bedroom door. As I fold myself into bed, press my cheek into cotton sheets and my hands onto my ribs, I realize I want someone to undress me until I'm bare, then warm me with touch from crown to soles. I imagine this happening until I'm calm. Abel plays video games all day. The first anniversary of his mother's death has just passed.

TIME SLOWED AS THE PRIEST PRAYED. I got lost in the roaming undulation of Hindi, the stress at the end of sentences pulling me up for air before dropping me into pools of vowels. The warm, oily water kissed my knuckles and swirled against the palms of my hands. It seemed as if we were finished when he stood.

"Wait. I know a Hindu god," I told him. "Sarasvati."

Sarasvati—the goddess of creative power. He started a new prayer.

I waited for my hands to tingle, for goose bumps to arrive on my arms. I wanted to hear a clear and unequivocal voice say: *You will live a long and fruitful life, and its tragedies are already behind you.*

Even when he pressed four grains of rice above my eyes, the humidity making them stick to my head, I felt nothing new. After I paid him, he wound a braid of yellow and red thread around my wrist four times. This badge of initiation was a sign that I'd been blessed.

MY GYNECOLOGIST, AFTER LOOKING AT MY CHART, says the miscarriage wasn't my fault. I know this and his words don't comfort me. I want someone to whisper in my ear *It won't always feel like this* over and over until I believe it. It doesn't occur to me until a year later that this someone could be God.

⁂

"I TAKE IT BACK, I TAKE IT BACK." Shouts bounce off the sink in the closet-sized bathroom. My voice sounds disembodied, a stranger's voice screaming. Dizzy, I hold onto the walls.

Is this real? I look down through my open thighs and see threads streaming down the toilet, lace-clots blossoming in water. "Whatever I did, I take it back. Please, God, please. I take it back." I catalog all my sins—those I've committed and the times I've failed to act. I place my will into the ears of God. I demand to be heard.

WALKING AMONG THE MONUMENTS at the Peace Memorial Park in Hiroshima, Japan, I learned that when the United States dropped "Little Boy" on Hiroshima on August 6, 1945 at 8:15 a.m., children were walking to school carrying book bags and lunch pails. My friend Kyoko had pointed out artifacts and told me how, except for her grandparents, all her extended family died in the blast.

I CALL MY MOTHER. She is the closest thing to God.

"Why is this happening? Did I do something wrong?" She can't understand me at first because I'm bawling.

"God isn't punishing you, honey," said says. She starts crying, too.

I suck in and then expel the air with sounds that don't sound human.

"Maybe the baby is fine," she offers. For the last nine weeks I've nurtured this pregnancy with good thoughts even when I was throwing up in the toilet and dry heaving into garbage cans in my office. I reject her hope. I know this pain.

"Does God hate me?" My voice has the tenor of a child's.

"Sweetheart, God loves you," she says, and I feel her love, complete and unconditional. On some level I know she's right even as a quiet voice inside reminds me that my version of God spun the beginnings of Life and then moved far, far away.

I take a deep breath when my mother promises that—from any angle we look at it—I didn't deserve this a third time.

IN HIROSHIMA, AN ESTIMATED 140,000 PEOPLE perished by December 31, 1945 and scores more died later from related illnesses, including twelve-year old Sadako Sasaki, who developed leukemia in 1956. After her diagnosis, Sasaki started folding origami cranes: "I will write Peace on your wings and you will fly all over the world," she said. In her honor, thousands of three-by-four-inch cranes, mailed or presented by children, are gathered each day by museum curators into display cases that decorate the Memorial. Children used plain and patterned paper for each crane: navy and baby-blue striped, black-and-white checkered, pinwheels of pastels, floral bouquets, fields of stars, tie-dye color bleeds. And then they strung the birds into two-meter-long garlands, some single hued in turquoise, orange, magenta, neon green; others alternate in patterns: two scarlet, three violet, two emerald, repeat. Sasaki completed 644 cranes before her death. Did each press of paper purge a cell of cancer? Did each turn of wing lighten her labored breath? Or did she pray to accept her fate, to surrender to God what had in store?

I CALL ABEL. When he gets home from work, he finds me on the toilet rocking back and forth. He coaxes me off, and he holds me in his arms. We talk about the future for a few hours between fits of tears. That evening, at the hospital, I learn no fetal heartbeat exists. The ultrasound shows it stopped growing three weeks ago.

The nurse gives me a hospital gown and instructs me to remove my contact lenses. Pictures on the windowless walls blur as they wheel me to surgery; I sense only the seat—covered with several layers of gauze—cushioning my skin. They wheel me down to the cold surgical room to scrape everything out. The image of carving pumpkins flashes, the stringy insides connecting seeds to the squash's thick walls. My core empty again.

CHILDREN FROM ALL OVER THE WORLD offer ten million peace cranes each year. Some crane-wings turn out in flight, others' wings flat against their paper backs, resting. The most pure and innocent and selfless as prayers come—the prayers of children. Yet someone collects these over-flowing shapes of children's prayers. Then do they burn them, the prayers floating in the air as ash?

❧

IN PUSHKAR, THE PRIEST HANDED ME a coconut small enough to fit in my palm and he asked me to repeat his words. Mine tumbled into the nut through a crack and fused with its sweet flesh. I couldn't have known that my ego should've spilled with the white milk into the lake water as I poured it. I couldn't have known that the emptied shells sank and joined a feast of prayer.

Not anticipating a prayer's answer is easier when the only thing at stake is the re-weaving of one's own body of knowledge, not the unraveling of one's own body. During miscarriage, what had divided and what had implanted and what had connected untwisted. The flesh-of-my-flesh disappeared. Grief obscured everything and everything was grief.

I've been the yellow string and I've been the red string; I've been the opposite ends of an origami strip and I've been split into two red threads. I've been strengthened by being pinched, stretched, and twisted, and I've been unraveled by the tension. I wanted to understand the meeting of water and milk and to comprehend the lift of ash onto the wings of a breeze; I studied breath of wind moving through the trees and I needed to believe the wind moved through me.

My bracelet from Pushkar—cut from my wrist for safekeeping—marks my page in a book of prayer. Each time I open it, I imagine syllables transforming me as they fly from my lips on a great wind. I grasp this thread of words, accepting I may not even recognize them when, or if, they return.

Once Upon a Tower

NOVEMBER 9, 2009

"Do you want to climb the Campanile today?" I ask Holden, my son.

"Yes!" he shouts, pushing open the door of his preschool. His hood slips off revealing hair brown as mahogany and just beginning to coarsen, a shift in texture. This seventy-degree November day in South Dakota transports us back to late summer. Had I known that winter would bring Holden's first epileptic seizure in its icy hands, I would've wanted to stay in that magical day forever.

"Wait," I say. I snag his shoulder just as he steps into the parking lot. "Look both ways."

"Okay, Mommy." He pauses.

For weeks, he's been asking to climb the Campanile, which rises from the Sylvan Green at the university where I teach. His teachers told him that he could see far, far away from the top, as if the Highway 14 bypass and farmland to the north was a fairytale landscape dotted with beanstalks and cottages, the houses to the west and campus buildings to the east made of iced gingerbread. The breeze blows across this flat land, a grass-rippling wind that once morphed the tall-grass prairie into an inland sea. Inside the Campanile, however, the air is musty. Filtered sunlight illuminates bits of lint and dirt that drift and swirl as though spent pixie dust. The room seems to shrink until I look up.

Cement staircases zigzag to the top, one hundred seventy-nine steps floating unattached to the tower's walls. My calves tighten; my feet feel rooted. Yet, when I examine the staircases, I see rods holding sets of stairs together. A sturdy spine. I exhale my held breath. Holden is already five steps ahead of me. As I catch up, shoes scraping against the cement, the eighteen-inch space between the thin railing and stairs gapes at me. A child could tumble down, fall through. An image of Holden's foot slipping through bubbles up, and I blink it away. Fear reappears, moving from the pit of my stomach along my limbs. My feet tingle. I lock hands with Holden and I pull him close.

Turn a few worn months into this story, and I'll fall from normalcy. I'll look over my shoulder from the kitchen sink, wrists wet and sudsy from washing off birthday cake from plates, and I'll spot Holden curled up on the couch among a cornucopia of new gifts. I'll decide to rouse him, to tickle and shout and shake him, time slowing until I'm just staring at his chest, unable to tell if he's breathing. I'll plunge into panic. A spell can look like sleeping with open eyes, but I won't know this yet. For a year, I'll be trapped in a tower of dull fear that Holden's preschool teacher won't respond to a seizure correctly or his daycare provider won't see him slip into one while napping or I won't hear him struggle to breathe over the baby monitor that I've put back in his room.

"Holden, we've gone far enough," I say. We're only halfway to the top of the Campanile, but my body feels like it's pitching forward, as if the floor far below is drawing me down like a magnet. "Let's go back down," I urge, tugging his hand.

"No!" he replies. "All the way to the top!"

"I'm a bit afraid," I say, squatting in front of him to look him in the eye. "We're pretty high up."

"Don't worry, Mommy," he says. "Just keeping holding my hand. You can be brave." In January, I'll say almost the same thing to him in the emergency room as a nurse inserts an IV needle into his thin arm, a post-seizure precaution. And that seizure will transform my usual parental fears—flu shots, broken bones, bouts of poison ivy—into simple concerns. To cope with elevated fear, I'll build escape plans for safety: strict sleep schedules, emergency medication in my purse, constant monitoring when illness lowers his seizure threshold, careful observation when he "spaces out," and the nearest hospital identified wherever we are.

But for now, I simply nod to Holden in affirmation. I don't want to transfer my fear, and I want him to trust me. Stories like ours should have heroes and happy endings, so I smile and steer us to the center of the staircase.

At the top, Holden gazes out a window as if it's a crystal ball. We watch the toy-sized students below. Perhaps he feels like he's morphed into a storybook giant or knight. Perhaps he claims the blue sky and green grass, the sidewalk bricks fanning out across campus as part of his kingdom. At the top of his tower, possibilities are unlimited.

"Everything's small," he says. "And look at this spider web! Ooooohhhhh." He squats down, finger extended.

I glance his way—he's safe in the corner—and I look out. The branches on bare trees stick out as if they're veins of the body, perhaps capillaries of the brain and lungs. We linger only until nerves overwhelm me. I conjure an image of us walking out the Campanile safely, and I focus on it while Holden and I step down the stairs one at a time.

MAY 10, 2011

The Aer Lingus plane has been in the air for only an hour when I start rocking in my seat.

"Look, Mom! There's a shamrock on the wing," Holden says, pointing to a graphic of the plane. He looks out the window to see if he can spot the actual wing. Not finding it, he relaxes back into his chair. "Can I watch a movie?"

First I direct the vent toward me to stir the stale air, then I fumble with his headphones. I cross and I uncross my legs. I push my back into the chair.

I resist the urge to sprint down the aisle and fling open the door at 37,000 feet.

I don't imagine what would come after: step off, free-fall, contact. I wouldn't take Holden with me, but wouldn't the plane's plummet surely follow mine? That question traps me further within steel seats, between a narrow aisle and a man whispering Bible verses probably aimed at me, the crazy woman shifting back and forth, squeezing shut her eyes, willing away her fear. I try to dissolve images of disaster. I draw a breath deep into my lungs. I try to loosen my stiff muscles that constrict me even tighter within the wind-battered plane.

Get a grip, I tell myself. Too late. My fear isn't embodied in a wicked witch, fanged monster, or corrupted king; it's simply the poison of panic. I felt it twice the month before. The first time I slipped into a window seat on a flight to Atlanta and, as if the panic had passed into my body with a bite of tainted apple, my heartbeat quickened. Nausea followed. My anxiety eased when someone offered his aisle seat near the cockpit. *A bit of flight-induced claustrophobia*, I told myself. *It won't happen again.* But the spell took. The next morning, I noticed a missed call from Holden's school on my cellphone. *Why would they call and not leave a message?* I wondered. *Perhaps they didn't want to leave alarming news on my voicemail.* The room shifted, tilted. When I called back, no one picked up, and by the final ring, sweat was beading off my body. I imagined kicking off my pumps and sprinting to South Dakota. After I learned that Holden just didn't feel well, I wondered. Without claustrophobia as an excuse, what did my panic mean? *Perhaps I'm starting to lose it*, I thought. *For those few seconds, I didn't feel in control. Maybe this is how a nervous breakdown begins.*

When Holden slips into a seizure, he loses anchor to the world. Some describe it as an attack, a good vs. evil brain battle. It's as if the shimmer of a magic mirror draws him in, and when he touches its liquid surface, ripples move through the nerves to his brain. Synapses surge in his temporal lobe, and the wave moves out. His conscious mind stumbles off some precipice. He could fall backwards off a chair or a swing. He could pitch forward and crack his teeth or bust open his chin. Once, people thought gods or demons caused seizures and only special rituals could cure epileptics. And despite modern medicine, the magic of how Holden's brain functions—or stumbles—is a mystery. Until one of his seizures resolves, I must protect him.

The cool air doesn't quell my desire to break out of my skin because what pitches me beyond the railing of tingling-fear, the end-of-a-cliff fear, is a memory of Holden on the bathroom floor with his eyes locked open, jaw locked shut, vomit forced through his nose—his last seizure in May three years before. The scrim between memory and reality thins when I panic, overlaying that image with that of him here, black headphones curled over his ears, giggling at something on the chair-back screen. My heart shakes its fist: *If he seized, what could you do? What would you do? What could you do? What would you do?*

In this tower of fear, I teeter at the top, grasped in double vision. Reciting my litany of safety precautions fails to calm me because by taking this flight, I've dismantled them: Holden's sleep will be disrupted, air travel increases his risk for sickness and thus lowers his seizure threshold, and no medical specialist can be rushed in. It seems rational that Holden could die because I'm not controlling every factor in my power.

My heart beats like a metronome with the weight positioned at the bottom of the slide. Dizzy, I head for the bathroom. Occupied. Between the escape door's big red wheel and the galley where the flight attendants prepare snack carts, I stand. One of them notices my tears.

"Are you okay?" she asks, maneuvering to stand squarely in front of me.

"I'm fine, really." I wrap my lavender cardigan around my waist. "I just have some anxiety when I fly."

"Are you traveling with someone? Do you want me to get a family member?" When she turns her head to scan the rows, I notice her curls are pulled back into a chignon, their dark color stark against her snow-white skin.

"Yes. But no—I don't want my son to see me cry." Out of the pocket of her green uniform, she pulls a soft pack of tissues, whisks two out, and hands me one. "I just feel so silly," I stop myself from adding *because I know that I'm irrational to fear my child dying from a seizure on this airplane*. If I do, she might point out the statistical improbability of a parent outliving her child, logic weakened by a memory of my mother kneeling in front of my sister's casket and the image of the first boy I'd heard about who died of SUDEP—Sudden Unexpected Death in Epilepsy. I recall Holden's bluish lips during his first seizure when death seemed close.

"It may feel silly, but that doesn't make the fear any less real," she says, looking me in the eye. "I can work in an airplane some thirty-thousand feet in the air, but I can't go up the Eiffel Tower without hyperventilating."

"Really?"

"Yes, I took my teenage daughters there on holiday a few years ago and had to hold them by their shoulders—like mother cats hold their kittens by the scruff—when they wanted to look over the sides. And there are railings there, too." Another mother has felt such impulses. I'm comforted by her candor.

"Why are you traveling to Ireland?" she asks me.

"Just vacation," I reply. "To wander around."

"Then I think you aren't silly at all; you have a lot of courage. You have this fear, but you're still here. A lot of people would just sit at home." Courage could be the antidote to panic, I think. I feel a bit steadier on my feet.

"True," I reply. "Thanks." I step into the vacated bathroom. As I lock the door, I can feel the spell thinning, the poison wearing off. I breathe deeply, dab the smeared mascara off my cheek, and smooth my hair with my palms. I look at the mirror and expect it to flicker or morph, but it just reflects me. Is remembering to breathe a form of courage? I decide it is, along with deliberate decisions I can make like choosing to walk back to my seat and watch my sweet son having fun on the flight.

MAY 20, 2011

With one hand clutching my hood and the other Holden's hand, I walk up the sidewalk to the legendary Cliffs of Moher, seven hundred feet above the Atlantic. When billowy white clouds move to reveal crisp blue sky, the colors below shift, too: a pasture of deep green lightens to sage; a charcoal-colored cliff face changes to copper, and the aquamarine sea switches to royal blue. Where wind meets ocean, it scoops up waves and slaps them over the rocks. White spray crashes upon cliff walls and then the powerful wave/wind combination twists, swivels—as if from a wrist—and spirals the mist up, up, up. The wind as hand. I wince, re-membering my friend's tale of a teacher from Spain who, when lecturing to her students on Irish history, stepped beyond the barrier. A gust blew her off the Cliffs.

"Look!" Holden yells. He runs beyond me. At the concrete barrier, he lifts his foot as if he's considering a climb.

"No!" I say, grabbing his shoulder. "Too dangerous." Holden shrugs off my hand but turns away from the barrier. I relax until the wind sweeps down from the direction of O'Brien's Tower. Holden spots its gray, crenellated stones—a lopped-off castle top placed at the Cliffs' highest point.

"Let's go to there, Mommy!" He wants to ascend. Barriers. Walls. Rock faces. Steps. Ladders. He aspires up, up, up. Holden weaves between tourists toward the Tower.

Once upon a time, a twenty-six-year-old woman, Eileen M., visited the Cliffs on a suicide-homicide mission. Witnesses say she bent down to hug her four-year-old son, Evan, then grabbed him, pitching them both over.

Hold on. Hold on, I imagine her saying. My instinct, like Eileen's, is to keep my son close. And I understand the glimmer of irrationality, the split second when the plunge feels more acceptable than the surging panic. That's where I stop relating to this other mother. I've held on to Holden for his life, for my life. My fear lasts only moments, not the days the Irish newspapers reported Eileen took to plan death: the one-way train tickets, the creation of calm reserve other tourists said they saw on her face.

Inside O'Brien's Tower, I pay my Euro at the gift counter; the clerk lets Holden climb for free. Two sets of stairs spiral up—each one tight iron with steps so narrow they barely accommodate an entire foot. Even Holden's. He steps onto the first tine, then turns and raises his arm. He wants to hold my hand and I want to hold his entire body.

Where fear is this high, I consider ways to come down. Towers tilt and topple, shake and crumble, blaze and explode. Filled with fear, the people trapped within them run, burn, fly, fall, or emerge. In our favorite stories, heroes help. Fairy godmothers transform fear, frog-trapped princes remove fear, and noble woodsmen negotiate it. At the top of the towers Holden and I face, I've tried to be the hero. I consider trying to talk him out of the climb for his own safety, which the glimmers of panic encourage.

Yet I know where irrationality took Eileen. Did she frame herself as hero, saving her son from a life of pain and uncertainty? I have no idea if Holden's epilepsy will spiral him up or down either path. But the flight attendant offered a new point of view: courage. I want Holden to feel courageous also, to know what to do when he steps out of a spell, and how to walk in the world with confidence. Holden, I realize now, must became his own hero.

"We can't hold hands this time," I say. "You'll need both to keep you steady." Despite seizures, despite a CAT scan and MRI, despite midnight ambulance rides, despite blood draws and heplocks, despite an anxious mother looking for spells, excitement still competes with fear. He hesitates. Should he trust his mother who has admitted to being afraid? The one usually demanding handholding but who has now switched her story?

"Hold on to the railing with both hands," I insist.

He decides to trust, as Evan might have when Eileen pulled him beyond the barrier. Holden bounces up the stairs. I walk up behind him, positioning one foot at a time. At the top, I snap photos of the Cliffs. Holden traces the paths of seagulls surfing gusts of wind. He waves at the people below.

"Let's go back down!" he yells. Wind whisks his words away.

Holden remembers to grip the railing with both hands, but three steps down the first flight, Holden's sneaker slips. I imagine his foot caught. Broken ankle, broken leg. When I reach out to him, I untether myself. The awkward angle pitches me forward. Holden slides down a couple of steps. I picture his leg catching, his torso twisting, his head smacking the railing. Worse, him tumbling forward, cracking his head open on the rock floor below. My hand lands on the opposite railing. I'm frozen, trying to untangle the angles and distance between us.

Holden grips the railing and he catches himself. After a pause, he looks back and smiles.

"Good catch!" I say.

"Thanks, Mom!" he replies, inching down the rest of the stairs step by step.

Once down from the tower, I'm no longer imprisoned, but walking on solid ground doesn't diminish my fear. Like Holden's epilepsy, fear is a breeze threatening to become a wind. I feel it on my skin, and I know it's always ready to reveal a new precipice.

Once on level ground, Holden runs out against the wind and starts to spin, his arms open wide. I breathe the crisp air deep into my lungs, and Holden twirls around and around on the cobblestones beneath his feet.

Priests

PALM WRAPPED AROUND THE MUG, I sipped my coffee and seethed. At the next table, three young men sat around a Bible, its pages dog-eared and worn.

"Suffering stems from our sinful ways," the eldest said, his voice rising with each word. "The more we sin, the more we'll suffer." One listener leaned forward, while the other pressed his palms on his jeans.

I tried to tune them out. I tapped my pen, then crossed out and rewrote the same lines of poetry over and over: "When lightning storms along synaptic clefts, cells surge. / In the nightlight's shine, I've seen sweat-soaked hair, / a twitching cheek, my son's rigid body." My son, Holden, suffered during seizures. I wondered how these men suffered.

"So weakness causes suffering?" The one with sweaty palms asked. The eldest affirmed his question and started searching for a verse.

I didn't believe that Holden caused his own suffering; he was only five years old. In fact, nothing in my religious education linked suffering and sin like this, but I was familiar with the "let's blame the one who's suffering" game. Historically, epilepsy stigmatized people. Morally depraved, some folks said, a self-styled suffering brought on by lack. This often led to social isolation—and more suffering. Families tended to keep epileptics domestically incarcerated. Or worse, they sent their seizure-besieged children to live in institutions fraught with neglect and abuse. We are so often responsible for the suffering of others, I thought. Why didn't the coffeeshop preacher reflect on this for a bit?

With each sip of hot coffee, with each sentence about sin, with each rewritten line, a wave of frustration moved through me. The preacher commandeered the room from his café pulpit. I hated his cocksure dogma. I despised how he pinned responsibility for suffering on the ones who suffered. As if they invited it. As if they controlled it. As if they deserved it. I didn't know which fueled my indignation the most: the preacher who took pleasure in pointing blame, the religion which gave him authority on suffering, or the God who permitted so much pain. God the father. We his children. If I could, I'd wipe my child's seizures away with my will alone.

CHASING DOWN RESEARCH FOR A WRITING PROJECT on Catholic nuns, I stepped out of my car in a church parking lot in Nebraska City. The sun practically seared my skin, and my sundress straps constantly slipped off my sweaty shoulders. My anger at God hovered in my emotional landscape, intangible and exhausting like the humid air on that hot July day.

Father Cyza, the parish priest, met me at the door and led me through the rectory. He wore the ubiquitous black shirt, black pants, and white collar, but walking through his living quarters made him seem less like a stand-in for God as I'd been taught.

"It's been so sticky with it in the 100s every day this week, " I said.

"I'm glad the A/C's working," he replied. He turned and waved me into his office. "Please. Sit down." We took seats on opposite sides of a wide desk. I fanned myself with a notebook from my bag.

I told Father Cyza about my nun essay idea, and how I hoped an interview would jump-start my writing. Since I was a visiting resident at the local arts center, I wondered if he could describe the orders in the area, perhaps serve as an introduction.

"There aren't any nearby," he replied. "Might I be able to help?"

"The essay's about my obsession with nuns. My mom told me that one prayed me into existence. I'm not sure where the essay is headed...."

"There aren't any to interview in your home parish?"

"I don't really have a home parish," I replied. Father Cyza nodded. Soon our conversation made it clear that I had membership in a group he loved to engage: lapsed Catholics.

Had I obeyed the annoyance that rippled through my body as this realization dawned on me, I would've politely excused myself and gone back to my room in the arts center to work out my writer's block there. But familiarity kept me seated. Father Cyza reminded me of the guys I taught in Lincoln when I was a graduate student: brown hair cut close around the edges, light-colored eyes, medium build. I appreciated his open smile and kind face. I was curious where our conversation would take me. So I took a deep breath, sat back in my chair, and tackled his question that hung in the air: "Why don't you try Mass again?"

"My beliefs don't sync up anymore," I answered. It'd been years since I'd attended church, long before Holden was born, but now the most obvious reason was frustration. "Medical professionals assure me that Holden doesn't feel pain during seizures," I said. "But I know he suffers." I described Holden seizing in bed, seizing in his car seat, and seizing in the bathroom, each episode a rip in consciousness. Holden didn't have words for these moments, but as he emerged from them, I read anguish on his face. Stupor leeched the brightness from his eyes. And this was only the physical manifestation; I often wondered to what extent epilepsy caused him to suffer psychologically, too.

Father Cyza drew out details about me and Holden with good questions and genuine concern. Emboldened, I felt my voice rise.

"And nothing makes me angrier than when someone says to me, *It's God's plan. Or God wouldn't give you something you couldn't handle.*" Father Cyza nodded. I'd never encountered a more patient, nonjudgmental priest. In Catholic school, they always talked down to us with stale rules and prescriptive advice. "Even though I still believe in God, I can't worship one that plans the suffering of children. It doesn't seem much different than the middle ages when they thought epileptics were possessed."

As soon as I said it out loud, the dots connected. For millennia, people influenced by western culture considered seizures a disease caused by evil spirits. Although the Egyptians and Chinese beat Hippocrates to the insight that disruptions in the brain caused seizures, it took until the 17th century for medical professionals in the west to be convinced. I knew, of course, that misfiring neurons caused Holden's brain blips—I understood the scientific explanation. If it felt ridiculous to say demons caused seizures, didn't it sound just as absurd to say that God permitted them?

Father Cyza fished out paper from his desk, and he started to talk about suffering. We fell into the flow of dialogue. He lectured on St. Paul and Job, turning the paper every so often to illustrate his point with a diagram. I raised questions introduced by anecdotal evidence. He'd counter with a biblical story or church teaching. Sometimes he annotated a drawing with an arrow. And I spoke to those, finally asking why God allowed children to suffer. I wanted to hear his answer now that I'd come to a version of my own.

"Pain exists in the world; it's part of human nature. God doesn't punish children, but suffering is part of God's plan. It can give us the opportunity to follow Jesus' example." I caught myself rolling my eyes.

"Isn't a five-year-old too young to be tasked with that?"

Father Cyza leaned forward and he rested his hands on his desk. "Perhaps it's you, his mother, that can grow in hope and love through your son's trial."

"God's making my kid suffer so I can grow in faith?" I raised my eyebrows.

"Perhaps through prayer, you can reflect and find your relationship with God strengthened."

"Why would God permit my son to hurt so he could get to me? It sounds like a mafia drama."

Father Cyza held my gaze for a full thirty seconds, as if he was searching for the best response.

I looked away. Light filtered through the trees, softening the edges of the room.

"Hey," he said. "Let's take a break. Do you want a sno-cone?"

LONG AGO, IF INFANTS presented with seizures, communities often blamed their mothers. "Bad milk" (caused by their own moral weakness) poisoned the children. I felt like the coffeeshop preacher would've agreed with this theory, and even though Father Cyza didn't, his point made me wonder: What was my relationship to Holden's suffering? I was learning about epilepsy, reading about medications, maintaining my vigilance to keep him safe (while at the residency he was with a trusted babysitter and his father). But was there something on a spiritual level? Did I need this opportunity to deepen my relationship with God because I'd missed earlier, easier ones, like simply going to church? My desperation to pursue all routes of thinking tangled me up. I arrived at a "no" intellectually, but I found it more difficult to end emotionally.

Looking back, I don't think Father Cyza asked me to suss out a mystical cause-effect, but rather he encouraged me to not waste a spiritual opportunity. That made sense to me. I had long believed that reflection helped me make meaning from experience and made challenges more livable. In other words, if wisdom could be gleaned, a shred of goodness existed in an otherwise painful event. Sometimes this wisdom felt spiritual. But imagining that my relationship with God needed deepening as a result of reflection narrowed the possibilities of meaning making, so I was reluctant to view it as such.

FATHER CYZA AND I STOOD AT ANGLES in the galley-style kitchen crunching on shaved ice in paper cups; I leaned against the sink and he leaned against the cabinets. "This machine will be great for church fund-raisers," I said. Father Cyza agreed. "The coconut flavor tastes like a piña colada minus the rum." We both laughed.

As Father Cyza described his parish and its school, he grew more animated. He listed the challenges they'd faced and how he sought to meet them; he highlighted the successes his parishioners achieved in helping each other recover from floods and fires. For families who needed food and services, he connected them with assistance. He emanated even more warmth when talking about his sister and her children, who lived nearby. I wondered if Father Cyza suffered. I wondered if the suffering he saw became a venue for deepening his relationship with God, or if he'd feel the same way if his nieces and nephews were the children in pain. Of course he would, I concluded. He's literally dedicated his whole life to God.

We talked well into the evening and shared another batch of sno-cones. With each round of conversation—topics of which ranged from suffering to partnership to education to parenting—my dormant anger dissolved a bit more. Each time I narrated a story, named a fear, or noted a reason, Father Cyza engaged it. Finally, with no one to blame for Holden's suffering, I saw it for what it was: chance—one variation in the experience of being human.

Over Father Cyza's shoulder, I saw the moon through the window.

"Oh, my!" I said. "It's really late. I'd better get going."

Father Cyza smiled. "Yes. It's nearly 11:00." I'd been there for *hours*. I slipped my pen and notebook into my bag and took a deep breath. It had been ages since I'd lost track of time and felt a slice of serenity. This must be what the sacrament of reconciliation is supposed to feel like, I thought, recalling that afternoon in the third grade where I confessed my sins—fighting with my sister, coveting my cousin's Barbies—to a priest so he could absolve them. But that experience had been terrifying, so far from the comfort my teachers said it would provide. Now I had a sense of the comfort that comes from naming—not sins—but uncertainties.

I felt an odd stirring in my heart. I wanted to pray. But how? I knew I didn't want to recite the rote prayers of my childhood.

"Father? Before I leave, would you say a prayer for me?" I wondered, after all the doubts he heard me confess, if he believed I was worthy.

"Of course," he said. "Let's go to the church."

We left our conversation in the office and we walked across the parking lot in silence. Without the scorching sun, the evening felt merely warm. In front of the church door, Father Cyza fished his keys out of his pocket.

Moonlight cast deep shadows in the church's interior and illuminated bits of color from the stained-glass windows. Candles burned at the tabernacle and baptismal font. The church smelled like dust, wax, incense. The beauty made me catch my breath.

Instead of flipping on a light, Father Cyza walked toward the altar. We took seats, side by side, in the front pew. As I waited in the stillness, it became clear that my anger had indeed fueled my own suffering by misdirecting my emotions. It had drawn my thoughts away from Holden to a powerless place where nothing happened except my frustrated churning. Now that it was gone, I could work to be the best parent to Holden with more focus and discernment. I was about to say this to Father when he opened his mouth to pray.

His breath lifted his voice and his words gained density as he spoke. The prayer shared no qualities with the generic, scripted kind I'd known. Father Cyza composed it extemporaneously, referencing details from our discussion. His voice wrapped me and dissolved into my skin as balm. Without the heat of distracting anger, I understood that my new relationship to suffering meant I would do what I could to alleviate Holden's pain, and I would accept what remained. And I also knew I'd be given help too, even if it meant the simple pleasure of sno-cones on a hot day or the engagement of my intellect or the witnessing of what I carried. I meant that, despite everything, words could mean grace.

After he ended the prayer, Father Cyza and I waited until my tears slowed before we retraced our steps to the back of church and said goodnight. "You'll stay in my prayers," he said. I smiled, and a breeze tickled my shoulders as I waved good-bye.

Crucible of Dreams

MY FIRST HOUSE DREAM started with an ear-splitting crash—a car accident just outside my front door. As I reached for the handle, I realized I was dreaming. I don't want to see the crash, I thought, and turned. A kitchen materialized: refrigerator built for a linebacker, dual ovens, maple cabinetry, Iznik-tile backsplash. Just beyond it, I spied a conversation pit, movie screen, and marble fireplace. My books and my grandmother's tea sets were displayed on shelves. Out back, water bubbled up in a courtyard fountain and bunches of grapes hung from the garden's pergola. I woke up wondering if the dream foretold my future home, then I laughed out loud. College professors don't live in mansions and I didn't play the lottery.

For several weeks, dream images dropped into my waking life. Pouring tea recalled the antique sets. Eating fruit summoned the garden. Walking to my front door gave me déjà vu. I tried to solve the puzzle my subconscious offered by considering meanings: I should organize my place, I should reflect on my goals, I should shop for a new apartment. If I assigned the right interpretation, I reasoned, dream fragments would vanish.

Instead, as I completed a doctoral degree, gave birth to my first son, and launched a new job in a new town, more houses appeared, including a villa encrusted with gardens and an army surplus store in the basement of a 1960s ranch. The stages of my sleep were set with renovated lofts, street-level walkouts, and condos tucked in the elbows of skyscrapers. These years weren't easy ones, but the challenges felt familiar, and so the recurrence of house dreams added urgency to my curiosity. Did the house motif indicate a lack of perception? Was I not heeding important insights? I'd always plumbed the depths of how and why I know, curious about the effects of my knowledge, however limited. Now, it felt as if my dreams were crucibles, the houses fecund elements that I, the ambitious alchemist, could transform if I could find the right catalyst and the correct temperature for the heat of my scrutiny.

IN THE FUZZ OF WAKING, just as my brain catapults me into consciousness, the crucible vibrates. It sends its resonant hum down my spine and the rest of my nervous system responds—images from dreams encoded. Throughout the day, whether I'm teaching or writing or parenting, they wait to spark of awareness. But the alchemist seeks and procures, so I began to track my dreams' ingredients in a journal.

In one, my mother and I walked three flights of stairs to find a "For Rent" sign Scotch-taped to my ex-boyfriend's door. Inside, we discovered mounds of dirty clothes and a tower of rotting takeout. I also realized the whole apartment revolved. It seemed my dream congratulated me on leaving that ride of constant fighting; even good relationships are soiled by the inability to clean out and clean up. I thought my sharp interpretation would heat the crucible and the elements of my dreams would change. Not so.

In another, I walked through an abandoned main street with boarded up windows tagged with graffiti. A post-apocalyptic armory had been built near a house, and between them ran a conveyor belt of toys and bombs. Inside the house, my son and my friend's sons opened boxes of toys. A little girl, too, opened boxes of Strawberry Shortcake dolls and Barbies—my toys. Her face was fuzzy. When I reached to touch her shoulder, she disappeared. Because I yearned for a daughter, I thought the girl was the child I'd have someday, yet a friend suggested she could symbolize me. The alchemist considers all possible solutions, so I stirred the elements in the crucible again: a lost innocence? danger in a shifting world? a desire to play house or play war? The elements swirled, melting but not transforming. I hadn't found the catalyst.

My house dreams lacked the terror of nightmares, but some elements were charged with loss. My mom's parents' doublewide trailer divided like cancer cells, furniture floating inside bloated rooms. My dad's parents' home was hollow, stripped of love and light. These sets recycled themselves, appearing again and again. Given the weight of their number and heft of their symbolism, they felt like a haunting. And yet my childhood home where someone actually died—my sister—never appeared. I lived there for twenty-one years, yet I didn't dream of its birch trees, juniper bushes, and volcanic rocks. I didn't dream about reading Sweet Valley High books in front of the fireplace or watching Wheel of Fortune after dinner. I didn't dream about my bedroom's stuffed animal net or gingham bedspread. I didn't dream about how I abandoned my room for my brother's bottom bunk in the weeks after my sister died. I analyzed, but nothing in the absence seemed key.

BY THE TIME MY DREAM JOURNAL revealed five years of house dreams, transmutation seemed even more important. I needed to calm or resolve or pacify whatever was claiming my dreams, demanding my attention. So I signed up for a two-hour dream analysis seminar. An alchemist puts faith in process.

"Write about your goals today," the facilitator instructed the fifteen adults sitting in a semi-circle. I wrote: *I wonder about the power dreams have to influence the narratives of our lives. Dreams seem to be the primary means of communication for the subconscious mind—the impulses we are hesitant to name. What am I missing?*

The facilitators kicked off a discussion. I nodded in affirmation as one attendee described the vibrancy of her dreams, and I was shocked to learn that many people don't dream in color or rarely recall their dreams. Yet for many, dreams were self-generated texts ripe for introspection. When the facilitator shifted to introduce the main activity, I was nearly trembling with excitement.

"This is to make your dream mandala," she explained, handing me paper printed with three concentric circles. "You can use the mandala to represent your dreams and reflect on their meaning." With my charcoal crayons, I scribbled twenty-three yellow, green, red, blue, purple, and orange circles. The bright colors represented the vividness of my dreams, and the circles the cyclical return of houses. As I drew, I smeared some accidentally with my left-hand. That looked pretty, so I smudged all the edges to symbolize blurry dream images. My fingertips were covered with color, so I filled the margins with thumbprint whorls.

When we presented them to the class, I realized that I was the only one who took the word "represent" literally; everyone else sketched actual dream images.

"Yours looks like a stained-glass window." The facilitator pointed to mine. I explained my mandala. "Fascinating," she replied. "Dreams of houses indicate possibilities."

Possibilities. Not just possible interpretations, but possibilities themselves. I held onto that shard of insight, convinced it would lead to transformation. Perhaps a change in my waking life—as it related to the dreams—would be the catalyst I was looking for. I hoped that actual change would end the house dream cycle.

TWO YEARS AFTER HAVING OUR FIRST CHILD, my husband Abel and I tried to have a second, but over the course of several years I experienced a series of miscarriages. After my fourth, I dreamed that I stood in our bland bedroom with its beige walls and plain linens. A hallway led to a double-doored closet: on the left hung Abel's clothes—black, gray, and navy-blue shirts; on the right hung a toddler's wardrobe—pink, purple, and yellow dresses. As I puzzled over this, another hallway appeared which led to an enormous room with high ceilings. It, too, had two halves. The left was an orthodox chapel with gilded surfaces, burning candles, illuminated frescoes, and icons of the Holy Family. Its other half? A mini casino with slot machines, roulette wheel, and blackjack table. Incense burned, its smoke settling into my nose; the ring-ring-ring sounds of the casino echoed. I figured this dream represented pregnancy's relationship to faith and risk. Considering the power of possibilities—my new alchemic ingredient—I decided to be open to having a child another way: adoption.

Before I got far with that plan, I dreamed that Abel bought us two new houses. One resembled the generic style of our actual house, so I thought it symbolized our stable, lukewarm life. The other house burst with detail: oak floors, Tiffany glass, built-in bookcases, and carved staircase leading to an attic. There I saw Abel's boardgame collection and a bonsai tree. Perhaps this house meant possibility for more vibrancy, creativity, and deliberate design, I thought. Perhaps, somewhere inside Abel's heart he had tucked away his own possibility—something detailed and beautiful that he would soon reveal. The games—his joys of strategy and play—symbolized our future. But the bonsai? Grown with sun and water in rich soil, yet clamped and cut ...by whom? I never answered that question; I began to watch for possibilities in my waking life, eager to see the psyche of Abel unfurl before me and our life as a couple enriched. I imagined he'd take the lead in the adoption and we'd find a way to complete our family together.

But like generations of alchemists before me, I failed. I failed to anticipate the actual results of transformation, the slippery nature of interpretation and magic and dreams.

My last dream of houses occurred a few weeks before Abel told me that he wanted a divorce. Inside the dream, I stood inside my home surrounded by pools. Underneath skylights and next to floor-to-ceiling windows, the pools began in the living room, the first a foot in diameter, the next twice that size, and so on, culminating in an indoor swimming pool. Beyond the windows, four tall, thin-branched trees grew on my lawn. The branches were bare except for a handful of leaves budding at each one's tip. Tied among them were short cords that seemed to be aflame. I knew someone had tied these cords and set those fires on purpose. Instead of burning the whole tree down, though, the bundles extinguished. As I watched the tendrils of black smoke rise, I knew that Abel was responsible for striking the matches.

When I woke, I understood that any fire Abel set would simply end, and that I'd be protected by water and its potential to renew.

GIVEN THE SHOCK OF DIVORCE, I didn't realize that the house dreams had stopped for several months. In hindsight, of course, I understood my failure. I wasn't willing to consider all the possibilities for changes in my life—just those with favorable outcomes. Dreams didn't stop until my life changed in a radical way through divorce, a seismic shift in the house of my heart. I couldn't provide the magic to transmute the elements.

"Possibilities" was actually *it*, in its vagueness, in its infinite number, in its equivocalness.

But failure doesn't mean that the alchemist quits attempting transmutation. My dreams are always crucibles for my mind to engage. What burned away in the house dream cycle was pride in the certainty that I always be able to know, the part of my ego that told me I could figure anything out. Settling into the dimensions of my uncertain possibilities wasn't—and isn't—comfortable, but alchemy promises magic, the unexplainable, on its own terms and its own time. The work is being okay with that. Instead of a relentless pursuit of correct of interpretation, I appreciate the procuring, the stirring, the wondering without pressure. I like watching the bubbly, melting mix.

The next vivid dream I recalled after realizing the end of house dreams was set in the medieval village of Yvoire, France, which I'd visited as a teenager. As I walked from the docks of a placid lake into the town, I stepped through buttressed arches. The stones, pressed together, became the bones of buildings. The bottoms of my feet pressed the cobblestones. When I looked down to see the path, I saw that I was naked. I popped into a stationary boutique, browsed marbled scarves at a corner store, and sipped coffee at a café. I had no clothes, no money, and no shopping bags; still, I moved about the town as if I roamed nude every single day of my life.

Marriage & Marble

BEFORE YOU AND OUR THREE-YEAR-OLD SON joined me in Prague, I worked in Europe for two weeks without you. The separation from your hugs, from your sleep-filled breaths, from your chitchat over an evening meal, from your gourmet cheese omelets, from your memorized punch lines, from your presence in my bed, electrified my desire for your touch. You wouldn't walk the St. Charles Bridge with me at dawn—you preferred to sleep in—but we watched fog lift from the Vltava River, drank beer in low-lit pubs, toured hill-cresting castles, and followed a guidebook's scavenger hunt. "Like geocaching with art," you said. You led us down winding, cobbled road after winding, cobbled road until we saw all the listed David Černý sculptures: babies crawling up the Žižkov Television Tower, a statue of St. Wenceslas riding a dead horse, the two "peeing men" outside the Kafka Museum.

Despite the tourists lounging at outdoors cafés and queuing in serpentine lines outside the Old Jewish Cemetery, Černý's *Hanging Man*— Sigmund Freud dangling by one hand from a four-story building—took the longest to find. I would've missed the intersection of Husova and Skorepka streets if you hadn't scrutinized the map. How bleak Freud seemed there, suspended from the building, its burnt-orange pipes and gutters like veins against the building's buttercream skin. "It represents the human need to make the decision to live life or let go," you read aloud.

The sculpture that drew me in adorned Prague's park on Petrin Hill, a height to which we ascended via cable car. It wasn't one of Černý's. The male figure supported the female figure's shoulder with one hand, the other cupping her cheek; arms wrapped around his neck, she's sinking into the embrace, marble skirt pooling around his feet. They kiss as if nothing, not even the green lawn with its handful of strolling, rain-drenched tourists, existed beyond them. Do you remember kissing me in a deli the October weekend you met my parents? We'd finished our sandwiches and chips, still sipping sodas and chatting with my mom, when you slipped your arm around my waist, dipped me back, and kissed me long and deep in the middle of lunch rush.

Grabbing your hand, I pointed to the sculpture. I wanted that kiss. You wouldn't lean in. Not even to peck my cheek. Not even when I asked. I wondered if you loved me as this sculpted man adored his beloved. Now, I see love's end emerged here in the ways we moved, spoke, kissed, danced—or didn't.

"I FEEL LIKE WE'RE SPINNING away from each other," I said after we returned from Prague and I found the words. You sat on the deck stairs that hot July day, and I stood in front of the crabapple tree, many of its branches barren. Even though I lopped off those I could reach, from across the yard anyone could tell it was dying.

"You've been pulling away from me. Even before the trip. Hours playing video games, watching movies alone, checking your email until midnight. What's going on?" I grabbed a few leaves off a low branch, studying them for blight. None were curled or frayed. No leaves displayed spots or clusters of mold. I couldn't tell why some branches refused to bud, as if immune to the pull of summer's heat.

Your expression hardened. "What exactly do you want?" you asked. I didn't have the courage to say *to feel loved again.*

"I want to spend time together. Go on dates. Go dancing," I said.

I waited a few seconds, imagining you'd say, "Let's go out this weekend. I'll find a sitter." Instead, your eyes narrowed, gazing into the chasm between us.

"Nothing I do seems good enough," you said.

Impasse. The end of every conversation about us.

"DO YOU WANT THIS LIFE?" I gestured to my body, our bedroom.

You were angry because I'd asked you to help me plant my garden before I flew to Russia. You hate being outside, sweating and dirty, and

I know this, but I asked for an afternoon of digging so we could enjoy fresh beans, tomatoes, carrots, and squash. You gave me four hours on Saturday, but for the rest of the Memorial Day weekend, you avoided me by staying up late and slipping away to run errands. Exasperated, I confronted you.

From where I stood next to the bed, I could see the garden, the spiral structure for herbs at its center. Our five-year-old helped me lift the concrete squares to form its base, and he hugged armfuls of dirt to fill it in. In the following weeks, we watched our sculpture sprout basil, dill, oregano, cilantro, chives, parsley, tarragon, rosemary, and sage. He cut sprigs for salads, and he remembered how we planted the sand-sized seeds. You always forgot what we grew and returned from the store with herbs sealed away in plastic containers.

"Yes," you answered. "I want you."

For two years—since that Prague trip—I heard words come out of your mouth that your actions contradicted. *Yes, I'll go to the street dance*, but you sat on the side, even when other men tried to dance with me. *Yes, I'll go to the parade*, yet you listened to a podcast on your iPod and leaned against a tree, unable to hear our son's excited chatter, unable to see the happiness on his face as he caught Tootsie Rolls and Smarties thrown from the floats as they passed.

IN RUSSIA, I VISITED the Fallen Monument Park in Moscow with my colleagues. The park started after the collapse of the Soviet Union when Russian citizens toppled statues of Lenin and Marx, workers and peasants, and drug them—haphazard—here. Usually, curators shape the gestalt of the viewer's experience by making deliberate choices about how to place statues and metal sculptures in relationship to each other. And in the newer sections of the sculpture park, I could tell that the curator considered the dynamic architecture of landscape; how, for example, each piece in the newer section conformed to a hedge's bend, a hill's slope, or a boulder's angle.

You often sought such direction from me. You often said, "Just tell me what you want me to do" about cooking, tending the yard, planning a date night, whatever. So it went. If I asked you to clean the bathroom on a Tuesday, I'd spend three days ignoring the toothpaste speckles on the mirror and the grime lining the toilet bowl. On Saturday, I'd interrupt your videogame campaign. "When will you clean the bathroom?" I'd ask. You'd march off, emerging ten minutes later with the toilet, sink, and mirrors sparkling. But something would always be left undone. I wouldn't notice that you skipped the shower until the next morning when I'd see the ring around the porcelain tub. When I'd tease, "I think you missed a spot," you'd sigh, your gaze narrowing.

In the newer areas of the sculpture park, I found myself studying couples. One piece, *Minuet*, depicts two Victorian dancers, arms held up and locked, hand-over-hand. Such fine-chiseled costumes: the woman's fancy handkerchief and the man's detailed pockets. When I followed the gaze of each dancer and observed a neglected park—litter tumbling between installations, grass nine-inches long sprouting tufts, weeds creeping up pedestals—it was clear the groundskeepers didn't share the curator's meticulous care. I never wanted to map out the long-term dreams or daily directions for our married life; I wanted us to curate together.

Remember when you bought me dance lessons as a Valentine's Day gift the year we got engaged? Swing, salsa, foxtrot. I loved watching you pivot and step, your body's muscle memory retaining the poise and fluid motion from years of martial arts training. You had perfect posture—head up, shoulders back, elbow right-angled. Lean and muscled, strength swept you across the dance floor. You just needed to learn the dance sequences and how to communicate your intentions to me with pressure from your hand. Even when you looked away—toward the instructor, toward the door, toward the parking lot—I was supposed to understand your intentions by the turn of your hand. When you forgot, I anticipated the movement of your hips.

From the angle I snapped the photograph of *Minuet*, I notice the woman's arched eyebrows, her lips drawn into a pout. I can see only the back and side of the male dancer's body. Without his face, I can't see the hard gaze of disinterest.

DURING A BREAK OF WALKING in the Fallen Monument Park, I sat on a bench across from a twenty-something couple, close to our age when we met. I chuckled because I knew you'd make fun of their matching clothing: white t-shirts, white shorts, black sandals. The woman lay across the red-slated bench, head on his right thigh. She clutched his hand, as if she dreamed she needed to hold on tight, as if she felt his attention spinning away. On his left thigh rested a mini laptop computer; his left hand pecked out words. They fit into the park, as if planned. The man attended to the computer screen as a dance instructor would study the alignment of a student's heels and sit bones or scrutinize a dancer's plié to see if her scapula lay flat. I don't remember when you started to choose screens more often, two-dimensional games and movies an easy way to pass time. I wanted to approach the woman, to pull her to my bench and warn her, "Be careful, be careful." Instead, I photographed them.

When I saw a pair of marble figures beyond a smattering of shrubs in Moscow, I still believed work and creativity could renew our relationship. From a distance, one figure had long hair, curls flowing as if in defiance of the form. She knelt in front of a seated figure, his head in front of her hips. An intimate kiss. My breath quickened and my heart softened. I walked closer to see the expression on her face. From this new perspective, I could see that the male figure was kissing her smooth torso, and I recalled your lips against the stretched skin of my swollen, pregnant belly. Even heavy and tired and scattered by hormonal surges, I floated from moment to moment with you, the sharp edges of our lives (jobs and home in transition) rounded out. At night, with your arm over my hip, I felt an intense dimension of love—love triangulated with this person we'd created together. The shift in evening sunlight brought me back to the figures and my new understanding of our muted love.

A FEW WEEKS AFTER YOU SAY "DIVORCE," I sort my photos from Russia. I realize I photographed more than pairs. Among the couples, Alexander Pushkin sculptures, and busts of Stalin, three singles: *Child Hugging an Object*, *Man Alone*, and *Woman on a Bench*.

I scrutinize them. I wonder what it means that I photographed these statues. Was I trying to tell myself something? *Face your fear. Admit your family is broken, so broken that its elements can't exist in the same piece of art.* A wave of panic seizes my heart. Where another viewer of *Child Hugging an Object* might see the child's chubby arms, full cheeks, and bald head and say "adorable," I obsess about his posture: he kneels, sitting over his thighs, and he hugs a pillow almost his size; his eyes are closed, his lips drawn to a pout. Is this our son, heartbroken? I hope not. Perhaps *Child Hugging an Object* represents the past when our unhappiness burdened him. Perhaps the future will free him, too.

Man Alone's arms hug his knees against his chest. His curly beard and longish hair, however, ages him beyond your years. Cottonwood seeds blanket the blades of grass around the statue like snowflakes. Sunlight filters through leaves making shadows on the statue's back and casting his face in darkness. You say you want to live alone. I can't imagine this means happiness for you, now or ever. You don't curate life experiences, you just accumulate them.

I've sat the same way as *Woman on a Bench*, arms resting on her thighs, elbows drawn into her body as if she's cold. The sculptor carved her from rough-hewn rock and placed her on an unadorned pedestal. To her right, the bench is empty. Her face turns away from the space, chin resting on her shoulder. Her eyes are closed, lips frowning. She grieves the emptiness beside her. Yet the evening sun warms her face and the left side of her body, lightening the cement-gray stone. Her toes are pointed like a ballet dancer's. She's ready. All she needs to do is step away from the space into a new rhythm.

The Gnôsis Associated with Snakes

Behold, I am sending you out as sheep in the midst of wolves, so be wise as serpents and innocent as doves.
—Matthew 10:16, *English Standard Bible*

You were born with a snake in both of your fists while a hurricane was blowing.
—Bob Dylan, "Jokerman"

I WAS SENT TO FIND GRANDPA Welby in his garden—a half-acre plot cordoned off from the yard by six-foot tall hedges. I ran across the grass as fast as my four-year-old body would go, my two blonde braids flying in the air behind me. I opened a doorway through rough stalks of sunflowers to find him sitting on a bench, still like a park statue. On one side, bean poles. On the other, a trellis covered by orange trumpet blossoms. His long legs were crossed and his trousers were dusted in dirt. An elbow rested on his knee to steady his arm and the three-inch ash hanging from his Pall Mall.

As I stepped between rows of potatoes, I spied a snake rippling through the leaves. Cold fear gripped me. I knew snakes as serpents only, the kind that tempted curious girls in gardens.

I screamed "Snake!" Then, I froze.

Grandpa moved with unparalleled speed and he swept me away from danger. After, he wrapped me in his arms and carried me into the yard.

"Chrissy, garter snakes are good for the garden," he said. He placed me on the tire swing and gave it a push. The willow began to creak. I was one of the youngest of his twelve granddaughters; he'd spent many hours in this spot.

I looked up at him through my tears. He seemed more massive than 6'4," blue eyes shining against his jet-black hair, a modern-day Dagda. "They eat bugs, bugs that eat the vegetables." He spoke out one side of his mouth, cigarette still dangling from his lips. "They won't bite you."

Garter snake, not serpent. Good, not bad.

I chewed on this changing knowledge and the end of my braid as Grandpa pushed me higher.

HOLDEN, MY FOUR-YEAR-OLD SON, pointed to a garter snake in our driveway, a Z scooting across concrete. Teachable moment, I thought. I grasped his hand.

"Some people think snakes are bad. Sometimes, in books, they're the villains." I chose the perfect words to transmit this knowledge. We tiptoed closer to the snake. Holden pulled back a bit.

"Snakes can bite," he said.

"True. But not this kind," I replied. "I think snakes are powerful. They're important in nature and—" I paused. A few inches from my sneaker was the snake. Mid-length, something reddish pink seemed to be binding it. Then I realized its guts were seeping out.

"What's wrong with it?" Holden asked.

"It's injured. See, right there. That's not normal." I pointed at the spot. Holden squatted down to get a better look. Stock still, the snake flicked its tongue out. "What do you think happened?" I asked Holden.

He shrugged. "Maybe a cat ripped it open with its claw." I imagined the neighbor's outdoor menagerie of cats feeling happy, self-satisfied. I nodded.

"It's natural for animals to attack other animals, but I don't think the housecat intended to eat him," I said. "What should we do?" I tacked on the question more for myself than for Holden. After a few minutes of fretting over possibilities (Would we hurt it more if we tried to pick it up? Would a vet know how to sew it up?), the snake stopped moving altogether.

Did Holden understand what had just happened? I wondered how much I could say about life and death. Maybe just remaining calm would be best, I thought.

"It's dead, I think." I picked it up near its head; it didn't coil or respond. "Let's put it in a place the cats can't get at it." Holden pointed to a pine tree on the other end of the yard, the furthest point from the neighbor with outdoor cats. I laid it on the pine needles, inhaling their scent a second before covering the snake with a handful. "Too bad it died. Snakes are really good for our garden."

Holden nodded slowly, twisting a pine needle with his hands.

WHEN THE BOA CONSTRICTOR slid across my neck, it tickled. A giggle rose, threading the terror that locked my body, arms in the air, palms up. As the snake adjusted its length across my frame as the camp counselor said it would, a vibration pulsed along my skin. The reptile wasn't slimy as I'd expected but cool and soft and smooth.

Abby, a new friend, knew I'd need to be dared. The day before she'd persuaded me to go rappelling, and I sobbed the whole way down. And yet, as soon as my feet touched the ground, I turned to her and said, "That was amazing! I'd do that again." So when the counselor asked, "Who wants to hold the snake?" she'd grabbed my wrist, I whispered in her ear, and both of our hands shot up together.

The snake stopped moving when its head reached my right wrist, the other end draped around my left arm. I stood still, hypnotized by its beautiful brown patterning, until I switched places with Abby so she could have a turn.

Abby knew how to have fun, and she also knew Jon, the boy I'd hoped would ask me to be his date for the bonfire on the last night of camp. He always wore a blue baseball cap, and when he caught me staring at him, he'd tucked his curly brown hair underneath it. We'd both blush. "Why don't you just ask him?" Abby prodded. I shrugged. I didn't know how, and I didn't know how to find out how. The night of the bonfire, one second Abby and I were selecting the best log, and the next Abby and Jon had switched spots. We sang songs as the stars began to emerge and inhaled the scents of pine and smoke. After dark, when the ghost stories started, Jon slid his hand next to mine, tickling my wrist. Each time I felt his skin move against mine, a tingling uncoiled from my core and shot through me.

On our way back to the cabins, Jon grasped my hand and a giggle rose, threading the fear-laced excitement. I felt this vibration, ancient and primal, slither between us. And this, I thought, is how to know.

"THERE'S SNAKE AT THE DOOR!" Holden yelled. I turned from wiping down the kitchen counter and looked at him, eyebrows raised.

"Seriously! Come see." Outside, snow drifted waist-high, and despite the approaching spring, the weather showed no signs of thaw. Surely, I thought, he must be joking. But I followed my five-year-old down the stairs to the walkout basement, and sure enough, a garter snake stretched between the ends of the vertical blinds and sliding glass door. The image stunned me, and I blinked a few times to make sure it was real. Then I touched it, and the snake responded sluggishly.

"How did it find its way in?" I wondered. Had the warm interior attracted the reptile the day I'd shoveled a path for the meter reader? If so, how could I have not noticed? Holden remained silent. I opened the door a couple of inches, and cold wind rushed in and filled the room. I stared at the snake, hoping it would sense the change and move toward the outdoors, but nothing happened.

I grasped the snake on the spot where its head ended, unsure of my next move. It felt light, like a weighted ribbon hanging from my finger and thumb. What did snakes do in the winter? They must hibernate, I thought, imagining rows of snakes in burrows, hollow trees, caves. But none of that seemed right. I couldn't imagine them eating enough to survive all winter like bears. Dumbfounded and standing there with a dangling reptile, I wondered about the life cycle and lifestyle of snakes. I contemplated the daily cares of the living, breathing snake I held. I had only bookish thoughts, not biological knowledge. Snakes symbolized life, death, evil and fertility—depending on when one lived. They were associated with water, healing, regeneration, and the spirit world—depending on where one lived. They'd been central to the stories of humans for millennia. My understanding of my knowledge gap expanded. I didn't know where they lived in the winter, or where they were supposed to live. My basement didn't seem like a wise choice.

"I think it eats insects," I said to Holden. "There aren't any insects in our house." He nodded. I did the only thing that felt reasonable. I placed it on a snowdrift and closed the sliding door shut, imagining it would slide its way to safety.

After the snow melted and we experienced a proper summer, I prepared our house for sale. Holden's father and I had divorced the previous year, and we'd stopped using the basement when he moved out—fewer rooms to keep clean. And Holden, recently diagnosed with epilepsy, needed more care and attention. As I inspected every nook and cranny, I found snake skeletons in the basement baseboard heater. Fragile. Tangled. Were they the remains of baby snakes? Relatives of the snake I'd cast out? Then I realized my stupidity. Near the heater because they needed warmth. Cold-blooded. I'd sentenced that snake at the door to death. I couldn't bring myself to show Holden the knot of bones.

AT THE HERAKLEION ARCHEOLOGICAL MUSEUM IN GREECE, I studied the Snake Goddess, a fourteen-inch figurine with a cone-shaped dress, narrow at the waist, and open in the front, exposing her breasts. Snakes decorated the apron over the dress, and the head of a snake coiled around her tall hat, peeking over at the top. She stood with her arms open, palms up. Starting at her wrists, snakes wound up both arms.

I paced in front of the glass, excited. Six years prior, the summer I turned 18, I'd read a book that argued the Minoans had been egalitarian, women and men living in a more balanced partnership than any society we could point to today. The scholar cracked open other ways of being and knowing, offering different frameworks for interpreting history. Where did she muster the audacity to question what and how we know?

On a February pilgrimage to Crete, no matter where I seemed to be—sitting on the ground at Phaistos, feet dangling over unearthed clay storage jars, or sitting in a cave above Matala Beach, eyes scanning the ceilings for hippy graffiti—I felt time thin and the energy of the past well up inside me. Standing in front of the Snake Goddess was no different.

Some historians interpreted her as just some kind of fertility goddess, which aligned with typical paradigms of female images. Specialists associated the Snake Goddess with the domestic sphere since snakes were connected to the 'welfare of the Minoan household;' others saw her as a symbol of an underworld deity. But to me she meant beauty and power and balance. She was important enough to sculpt, important enough to save, important enough display. She didn't succumb to the snake's temptations; it didn't freeze her in fear. When I beheld the goddess and her set of snakes, it piqued a longing for mystery, for the knowledge she wielded.

I THOUGHT OF THE SNAKES as I dissembled my garden that summer I readied my house for sale. The realtor thought that its central location and the ever-growing compost area might not appeal to potential buyers. And what did I know about real estate? From my compost area, I yanked out a volunteer squash, its orange blossom yawning open. In my new place, there'd be no space for a garden, nor a big enough tree for a tire swing for Holden. And I'd started to see that Holden was having a hard time remembering and learning new things—even facts about snakes that we'd been reading about. I wondered if it had to do with his epilepsy or medication.

I tackled the compost with a pitchfork, dumping the rich soil into a wheelbarrow before moving it to my neighbor's back yard. Over the years, I'd felt the knowledges of brain and body, apprehended desire and creativity and fecundity. Once, in this garden, I'd synthesized knowledge by seeding and nurturing plants. But now I was learning that clearing a space to start over was just another point in the circle. As I got to the bottom of the compost, I displaced a snake. It slithered around the pile then turned, regarding me a moment, then its slim-ribboned body disappeared into the grass. This time, we'd both start over.

Disordered

HOLDEN, MY SIX-YEAR-OLD SON, stirs in bed. I hear a thump on the wall, bits of a song: "Sunshine, lollipops, and rainbows, everything..."

I walk into his dark room. "Morning, Sugar. You hungry?" "You hungry?" He matches my intonation. Flipping over, he smiles and pushes off his comforter. I plop down on the bed and wrap my arms around him.

"What do you want for breakfast?"

"Want for breakfast," he returns. I pull away a bit, looking him in the eyes.

"Break-fast?" I say.

"Yes!" Holden punches the air and breaks out of my arms.

"Omelet or pancakes?" I walk toward the door.

"Pancakes." He pauses. "I don't like pancakes."

"Omelet?" I look for recognition in his eyes, for understanding.

"Omelet!"

"Okay." My voice trails down the hallway.

"Mom! I'm hungry *now*!" He follows me. "I want pancakes."

I'M SIX YEARS OLD and already a language teacher. I chase my new classmate from Laos across the playground, zigzagging between groups of plaid-clad girls skipping rope. I grasp his coat. Looking back, I recoil at my behavior. This is the game: I trap him until he says a word in English. But which one? A jet soars overhead in the blue sky. I point to it. "Airplane," I say. Was he perplexed? Annoyed? Concentrating? Scared? I recall the deep shine of his hair: fine, straight, black. "Airplane," he says. I let go.

IN 1957, LANDAU AND KLEFFNER studied a rare loss of language in children with epilepsy. They suggested that persistent convulsive discharges in brain tissue largely concerned with language communication result in the functional ablation of these areas. Neurologists think interictal EEG abnormalities in Landau-Kleffner Syndrome underlie a disturbance in cerebral integration or the loss of the ability to process complex auditory signals.

Upon diagnosis, each of my closest friends point out the irony: the child of a poet loses language. I try to wrap my brain around it.

To hear and yet not understand.

"TEŞEKKÜR EDERIM," SAYS THE MAN queued in front of me at the Turkish Airlines counter.

"Tesh...tesh..." The word I imagine needing most while living in Turkey for two years is the longest word I've ever heard, and it only means "thank you." My confidence plummets. Six months ago, I donned a cap and gown and wondered what the exact translation of *summa cum laude* meant under my name and degree, "Bachelor of Arts." At the airport, I feel defeated before I ever step off the plane, walk into a market, or enter my own classroom.

"E-kür." He encourages me.

"E," I parrot. The sound feels like a burst of hot air in the back of my throat. "Koooor." I draw out the round vowel, copying his intonation.

"E-der-im," he says. Each syllable gets equal play, equal enunciation.

"E-der-im," I repeat. He claps my shoulder with his open palm. His daughter and wife look proud. The first of my many linguistic successes, I imagine.

A FEW WEEKS BEFORE FIRST GRADE starts, Holden's a pinball rocketing from bumper to bumper, room to room. In his bedroom, he throws over his Guy bin, Lego bin, Block bin, and Train bin. Batman and Iron Man drown in a mound of Legos; a pile of wooden cubes covers a caboose. In my room, he scoops up a handful of necklaces and throws them against the wall. Beads scatter, a few rolling under the bed. I unleash threats, and magnets on his positive behavior chart disappear one by one. A scene from Helen Keller's biography pops into my mind: Helen roams the kitchen snatching sausages from her family's breakfast plates. *Wild, crazy, wrong*, I think. On one course through the kitchen, he grabs a canister of sugar from the pantry and dumps it onto the living room rug. I have one logical strategy left: removal.

"Time out," I say, dragging a barstool into the middle of the kitchen and pointing to it.

"Hmmph!" Holden says.

"Now." My voice is firm, calm.

"No," he replies, kicking the pile of sugar. Crystals fly and land on the couch, television, piano. I feel the first flush of anger ripple through my body, and the muscles of my arms tense.

I pick him up. His body stiffens, arms at his side, legs straight. I lug him over to the chair but can't get him to sit.

"Fine. Bedtime. Go to your room." I half pick up, half push him toward his door.

"No!" he screams. "No! No!" He mutters a stream of garbled sound. I hear the word pajamas. I fish out some navy-blue shorts with white sharks from his dresser. "Nuh-huh." He shakes his head back and forth. Anger settles in my stomach. As I peel off his shorts and t-shirt, he throws himself on the bed. I wave the pajamas in front of him and he runs, naked, into the dining room.

"Why are you doing this? I don't understand," I say. The pressure of my breath tightens my chest. I have no words for his destruction, his intensity. I can't yet piece together these odd, erratic symptoms.

Holden backs up into the corner. My body looms over him, arms planted across my chest. "Why don't you just get dressed?" I screech.

He yells. I yell back and it feels good. When I stop, he looks up at me and blinks. Then he aims his penis at the open spot between his legs and urinates.

For two seconds, I'm stunned. The puddle grows. I try to reconcile what I'm seeing to the sweet boy I know, the one who helps his hurt friend on the playground, the one who says "please" and "thank you," the one who dispenses hugs like sneezes—free and compulsive and strong.

"STOP," explodes from my mouth. He doesn't. *Wild, crazy, wrong*.

I grab his arm and turn him around, smacking his butt with my open hand. A faint red outline of my hand appears.

Tears, shocked to the surface, run down both our faces.

MADAME DUBOIS MARCHES ACROSS THE KITCHEN and snatches the letter from my hand. I've spent three weeks in her care as an exchange student, hardly enough time for a seventeen-year-old to speak fluent French, and now she hurls it at me. The scene transforms the language I studied from worksheets and films—the language of cream pastries and stained-glass windows—into a frenzy of gauze. Her fingers scissor the air, tips pointed at my face. Wasn't the letter on the kitchen table junk mail? "Non, non, non!" Punches of sound. "Non, non!" The round ends in pressed silence. *Je regrette*, I manage. *Je regrette*.

IN LKS, EXPRESSIVE DEFICITS include reduced syntactic complexity, telegraphic speech, word-finding deficits, jargon, neologisms, paraphasias, perseveration, echolalic speech, and mutism. Articulation deficits, apraxia, and voice disorders also have been reported. If aphasia exists for more than two years, complete linguistic recovery is rare.

To know and yet not speak.

"HAVE YOU COME ACROSS LANDAU-KLEFFNER SYNDROME in your research?" Dr. Jones asks.

He cocks his head to the side, and I watch his crystal blue eyes scan the Pediatric Epilepsy Unit and zoom in on Holden, who is missing his fourth week of first grade to be here. My heart tightens as a calendar opens in my mind: eighteen months since I learned Holden's epilepsy entailed more than just obvious seizures; twelve months since I began to distrust his first neurologist's treatment plan; six months since I asked our family doctor for a referral to a proper specialist; three months of searching websites, skimming discussion boards, and slogging through medical articles. I tried to see my son in the jargon, in the matrices of symptoms, in the litanies of medications and side effects. *Wild, crazy, wrong*, I'd thought.

"Yes, I did. But I don't remember much about it," I say. "It was one of the scary ones." A flush of shame rises in my cheeks. Dr. Jones turns back to me and takes a deep breath. He does that a lot, a habit I interpret as weighing his words for balance, persuasion.

"Well, the EEG will tell us for sure," he says. "We'll talk more about it then."

Two hours later, I find a description of LKS on a website. I say "aphasia" and "agnosia" aloud, as if hearing them will reveal their meaning.

PERCHED ON THE STOOL, Holden pulls his iPad across the counter. One hand slides through his dark-brown hair, tufts standing straight up. The other hand dances across the screen. His eyes dart back and forth as he drags his fingertip down on the slingshot and launches a bird; mid-way across the screen, he touches its yellow chest and it explodes into three smaller birds that sail toward the stacks of green pig faces.

Flocks of syllables enter his perfect ear and activate hammer, anvil, and stirrup. They become absorbed by cilia and then—splat! Words fly. Some hit their targets in his brain's language center and walls waver, collapse; some soar way over the intended targets until they disappear altogether, lost.

IN ISTANBUL'S GRAND BAZAAR, Turkish swells in my ear. "El," "li," "lar," "lu," the soft "sh" and occasional "z" create a kaleidoscope of sound that turns the spinning world around me into mystery. Occasionally, I hear "Yes, ma'am," or "For Sale," or "Hello! Welcome! Hello!" in a slurry of syllables. When my group disappears in these capillaries of paths, the men who speak English phrases curb my panic. Among work-shirted salesmen and boys hawking tea, I wander this maze of jewelry shops and clothing kiosks, carpet stores and hookah boutiques trying to ask one question: "How do I get to the ferry platform?" Later, I'll understand their reactions: a smile, a slight head tilt, a furrowed brow—the strain of piecing words together.

When Holden's exhausted from the work of understanding or the work of finding words or the work of regulating the cocktail of medications he pops into his mouth twice a day, he weeps. His eyes glaze and focus on a window, book, or screen—anywhere but me. His lids relax. His bottom lip pushes out. His fist rubs out tears. And he cries a long time, sometimes the length of a grocery shopping trip or the length of a shower or the length of a meal of cheese quesadillas and applesauce.

WITH LKS, HOLDEN'S UTTERANCES SEEM LIKE CODE.

"I want to play mini-ninjas," Holden says, walking out of the bathroom with his jeans around his ankles. I can hear the toilet flushing behind him. "I want to play mini-ninjas," he says again.

"Pull up—"

"I want to play mini-ninjas." He pulls up his pants. I follow him around the corner. "I want to play mini-ninjas." He sits on the couch and looks around the living room. "I want to play mini-ninjas."

"We don't have that—"

"Mom, I want to play mini-ninjas!" I quick-list and associate: game, play, ninja-game, swords, a video game / any video game, dress-up with ninja costume, Bonzai Blade on iPad, ninja game he plays at his father's house, go to his father's house, see his father, read *Yoshi's Feast* because one character looks like a ninja. Holden wants something. My attention?

He grabs *Green Eggs and Ham* off the floor and opens it. "I want to play mini-ninjas. I want to play mini ninjas. Oh. Sam I am, that Sam I Am, I do not like green eggs and ham…." He flips through the book. No more ninjas.

"BEŞ," SAYS MRS. BORA. She holds up five fingers. On the train from Mersin to Tarsus, we toss Turkish and English between us and stories spin out from our words. Kids run down the crowded aisles dodging the legs of their dressed-up parents, squeals bouncing off the windows. Sometimes they stop near me and stare at the blonde *yabancı* in a short-sleeved shirt.

When words fail, we improvise with our hands.

"Five children," says Pinar, her teenaged daughter, keeping her spot in the dictionary with her finger. "Three brothers." She wears her hair loose; Mrs. Bora, in her early sixties, wears a gauzy headscarf with flowered fringes.

"Mustafa. Aydın." Mrs. Bora says, smiling. Then, she puts her hands together and rests her cheek on them, closing her eyes. "Ali…" She whispers. Her face softens.

"My brother," Pinar says. Her eyes look down when I catch them. She shows me the word "melek." Angel. I connect. Ali is asleep. Ali is an angel. Ali, the third brother, died.

I take Mrs. Bora's hands in mine and hold them. For a moment I'm convinced that words are superfluous.

"FUCK HOLLAND!" I SAY, clicking the document closed. Emily Perl

Kingsley concludes her famous piece where she compares the "change of plans" that parents must make when they learn they will raise a disabled child to planning a trip to Italy and landing, unexpectedly, in Holland: "If you spend your life mourning the fact that you didn't get to Italy, you may never be free to enjoy the very special, the very lovely things ... about Holland."

Even though she's right, with LKS I arrive in Japan one morning, the next Papua New Guinea. When I think I'm going to Montréal, I wind up in Bangladesh. Sometimes the day starts sipping espresso near the Eiffel Tower and ends on the streets of Bagdad. It'll happen. I'll land somewhere new and won't speak the language. At least Italy and Holland have a similar climate. Just tell me, I beg you, what to pack for this trip.

CONTINUOUSLY ABNORMAL DISCHARGES during sleep may also interfere with memory consolidation, and because they occur during a critical time of brain development, they may result in defective synaptogenesis and thalamocortical circuit formation. The potential impact of the persistent interictal discharges on brain plasticity is proposed as a mechanism for the resulting neuropsychologic impairment. Poor daytime alertness due to sleep fragmentation may contribute to the neuropsychologic deficits.

To sleep and yet not renew.

EXHAUSTED FROM THE WORK OF PLEASING his teachers or picking up his room or shampooing his hair, Holden sleeps. Tonight, his hands are folded between his cheek and the pillow. Oval, his brown teddy bear, hugs Holden's chin. My son's lips are full, bow shaped. His rounded nose extends up, flattens out between his bushy eyebrows. I can see the veins in his eyelids, the double rows of lashes curled.

AT FIRST, I IMAGINE THE SPIKE and waves affecting the language center of his brain as blizzards, flash floods, sandstorms. Chaotic spasms of nature. But now I turn that part of his brain into a warehouse of workers, and the cells don't sit at their desks in front of computer screens. It's a rave: a frenzy of lasers and liquid punk, tribal beats, neon shirts, glow sticks, vitamin-x tabs tucked under tongues. Find interpretive surfaces in waking life. In aphasia-house parties, dervish-cells spin off ecstatic. Not wild. Not crazy. Not wrong. They're ready for rapture, even if it destroys them.

INCREMENTALLY, I'M LEARNING AND RELEARNING. Kids queue at the end of Mrs. Stadler's first-grade line on the playground, wiggling under the weight of their Hello Kitty and Spider-Man backpacks. The line leader signals. Two of the six classes stream through the doors, one on the left and one on the right. Once through the double doors, the two lines split; Holden turns the wrong direction. Lily with the Sunshine Hair—what Holden called her before he learned her last name—wraps her arm around his backpack. And now, this girl whom Holden declared his love to in Kindergarten, smiles and steers him toward their classroom in happy silence.

A Study of Nuns, Light, and Love

NUNS

The presence of nuns in my life is mysterious and my persistent interest in them is baffling. My life began, so says my mother, because of a nun's prayer. Between my sister's birth and mine nine years later, a Catholic nun—a close friend of my grandparents—coaxed my soul into my mother's womb. The nun's prayers and my mother's love coalesced, and voilà: light in the dark space of my mother's womb. I have no memory of this woman who claimed me as half hers, but my mother raised me with the knowledge of mystical parentage, nonetheless.

As a first grader, I sat by Sister Monica Mary at Mass and mimicked the way she folded her hands in prayer. I tried to concentrate, but the stained-glass windows glowed like slabs of translucent candy. When the priest transformed a piece of bread into the Body of Christ, a soft light sparked inside of me. I closed my eyes, and when I opened them again, the sun had shifted: my classmates knelt beneath a rainbow's end.

The day after first grade ended, Sister Monica Mary and I ate sandwiches in her convent's kitchen. She gave me a mobile of spoon-sized fish woven out of pastel ribbons as a goodbye gift. Suspended on nylon thread from a delicate metal arc, each fish sported a plastic eye. On mornings when light bent its way around the catkins on the pussy willow tree outside my bedroom window, it filled the hollow spaces at the core of each fish and made them buoyant. The fish swam in a sea of sunshine.

Among my childhood collection of stuffed animals and Barbies were two nun dolls made by Sister Pacifica—my maternal grandmother's aunt.

Née Beatrice McNaney, Sister Pacifica was born in 1895, entered the order of Sisters of Charity of the Blessed Virgin Mary at 19, and taught primary school in Chicago and Montana until she died at 35. The dolls' habits were starched and dusty, and I loved to roll the tiny beads of their rosaries between my index finger and thumb. As I stroked their porcelain cheeks, I wondered how she made them and why.

In my mid-twenties, my friend Milaine taught me the practice of guided meditation to manage stress. "Close your eyes," she said. I welcomed the temporary surrender to the sunshine streaming through my apartment's windows. "Imagine that you are walking on a forest path. Very little sunlight makes its way through the trees…" I relaxed, imagining the branches, the brush alongside the path, and a clearing with a boulder in its center. I sat on the rock.

Then, without prompting, I had a visitation. A woman in a hooded cloak the color of blue asters approached me. When I asked to see her face, she said, "You're not ready."

My eyes snapped open. "Who's the nun in your life?" Milaine asked. "I kept seeing her watching over you as you meditated."

Eight years later, I visited Italy with my mother—a devout Catholic. I booked rooms at convents hoping to meet a nun who spoke English so I could strike up a conversation. Our room in Rome was so clean my sandals squeaked on the tiles and my fingertips, searching out the bathroom light, returned to me free of dust. The nuns had been there, scrubbing every inch, which comforted me when nausea sent me racing to the bathroom—my pregnancy with my first son at eight weeks. Nuns cleared and cleaned and cooked and disappeared. As if refracted light through a stained-glass window, they left traces of their care, not words.

LIGHT

Mysteries resist explanation, but they invite obsession. A nun praying me into existence, the fish-mobile making me feel buoyant, meeting a nun during meditation that my friend perceived as well: mystery doesn't conform to the ways I usually understand. But sometimes, if approached obliquely, I make discoveries. The light in the imagined womb, the stained-glass windows, woven fish dangling in the sunrise, low light in the forest, and the clean light of Rome—in all these images, the element of light suggests itself as a way of understanding.

As a child, I knew these sources of light: candle, fireplace, light bulb, sun. The candles at church: tall Pasqual candles, Advent candles, the stubby red candle at the center of a Christmas wreath, the rows of short flames near the baptismal font. Reading books by the fireplace in the home I grew up in, I occasionally stared into the glowing pieces of orange wood, white ash falling off. To change a light bulb, I imitated my mother, rocking a loosened one back and forth to see if it was burnt out or just screwed in wrong. Eating breakfast in the kitchen, I watched the sun as it appeared on the roofs of neighborhood houses, and I studied the sun's outline on the pages of my science book, a yellow splotch with a bracelet of planets on the wrist of the Milky Way. I recall learning something about light traveling as a wave, about travel between planets taking light years. I imagined that light moved on lengths of clipped yellow yarn, a magic carpet of sorts, invisible to my eye. Now I see the same yellow yarn in my son's blanket. It's the same hue as the floss he used for the counted cross-stitch he'd tried before seizures began to disrupt his sleep and focus.

The presence of nuns feels like light: illuminating, powerful, mysterious. And yet I wonder about that metaphor. Light is a physical phenomenon. Scientists have explained its mystery, its behavior as both a wave and a particle. In 1801, Thomas Young passed sunlight through a pinhole with two slits; when they hit the film on the other side, the wave nature of light caused interference, resulting in bright and dark bands on the film. The Pinhole Test confirmed conventional wisdom— light behaves as a continuous wave. And yet a hundred years later, Albert Einstein proposed an alternative way for light to behave—as a particle, a photon—because knew that electrons are dislodged if light reached or exceeded a threshold frequency.

And so, I experiment. I direct light through the pinholes of my observation, and what shines forth in the blurred space between? Love. Then, as if some threshold has been reached, as if an electron ejected from some mechanism in my brain, I see how light vibrates with love.

LOVE

I understand love conventionally, its wave-like dimension clear. I felt the hormone-induced love for my son, Holden, when he was born; how logical it felt to love that little moon-faced being, flesh of my flesh. I parented him on a scale I knew, one I could sense—teaching, playing, tending. Holden liked to explore cause-and-effect at preschool, so we donned lab coats and conducted experiments with baking soda, water, and vinegar. He enjoyed dumping sugar into bowls, so we mixed cutout dough, baked the cookies, and decorated them with yellow and red sugar sprinkles. He wanted to practice his letters, so we made homemade Valentines for his preschool class with stamps and stickers, and he wrote their names himself. He got cranky in the late afternoons, so we relaxed on the couch listening to music.

And then, when he was four, Holden was diagnosed with intractable epilepsy and, two years after that, Landau-Kleffner Syndrome. His cognitive skills, especially his abilities to use and understand language, regressed, and the pervasive seizures left him chronically in a fog.

Sometimes, during the sleep-deprived murkiness that made it tough for him to function, Holden hit or kicked me. Once, when he didn't want me to turn down the volume on his iPad, he hurled the charger at me, leaving a tiny welt on my back. With the onset of puberty, the fog lifted long enough for light to emerge. As the seizures abated, he learned to express his needs and thoughts with words.

LKS taught me that my theory of love wasn't sufficient; it helped me discover its particle-like ways. I learned to ignore the moments when he shoved plates of French toast onto the floor. I learned to anticipate his needs, and, when I failed, I learned to shepherd him to his room before the tantrum began. I learned to move in for a hug before Holden could hit me. None of these moves made sense conventionally, but love illuminated new paths for me to follow.

Not long after I triangulated nuns-light-love, I visited an historic church as a tourist. When I opened the heavy door, I gasped: sunlight from clear-paned windows drenched the interior with brightness, light bouncing off the ornate marble and metal altar. White walls culminated in a vaulted ceiling. And I caught my breath when I saw her: a habit-wearing nun in her mid 80s, kneeling at a wooden pew, hands folded in prayer. She barely moved, and I barely breathed.

Nuns dedicated their lives to God. Put another way, they dedicated their lives to love.

I wept silently. A nun had prayed me into existence. If this one here prayed for Holden, could her words accomplish with mystery what my will and love could not?

Although I've never stopped wishing for the impact of the seizures to disappear, my answer is no. And not because I've lost faith in mystery, but because nuns-light-love helps me understand the ways that love powers and empowers me.

AS I'M REVISING WITH THIS ESSAY for what feels like the last time, a former student, Catie emails me with an invitation for tea. She'll be moving to California to reunite with her husband after finishing school and wants to say good-bye. We're settling in with our cups of chai at the public library, a muted winter light bouncing off the snow outside, when Catie sips, puts down her mug, and looks directly at me. "You know, I chose an unconventional path after high school."

I sit forward in my chair, ready for a good story. I imagine Catie trekking through Mongolia, waiting tables in Las Vegas, or living an artist's life in Seattle. Instead, "I was a nun for eight years and lived a cloistered life, first in Alabama and then in Arizona." Catie brushes her dark hair away from her eyes and reads the look of surprise on my face. I couldn't get over the serendipity of yet another nun, one I didn't even recognize the whole semester. Even though Catie often spoke in class, she rarely shared personal details; there was always a veil of mystery about her.

But that seems to be the pattern for me: nuns, light, and love—even when I least expect them. Mystery and understanding comingle and yield a new way of loving.

And when I received Catie's blessing before she left South Dakota, a loving prayer bound in words with the promise of light written on a hand-made card (and accompanied by a candle), I recognized how love empowers us: *I wish you greatness in your art and skill, joy and happiness in your family, and health for your blessing—the life of a son and the wonderful impact your love and his presence cultivate in our world.*

Culinary Alchemy

WHEN SPECIAL GUESTS ARRIVE IN TOWN, I cook. At midnight on Friday, I roll out egg noodles to dry, the chicken already boiled and deboned. Saturday morning, I bake rolls and select the apple cake recipe. By late afternoon, I've baked that cake and I've cut carrots and green beans for a side dish. Two of these recipes are my mother's staples, but two are new, concoctions I've snipped from magazines along with thousands of others. I cut lists of ingredients for Provençale Kebabs and Tomato Basil Soup; directions to mix, spread, and layer for Pumpkin Lasagna, Enchiladas Florentine and Chocolate Banana Loaf; substitution suggestions for Wild Mushroom Ravioli; preparation details for Braised Tofu and Quinoa-Stuffed Squash. A *bit of this*, a *dash of that*, *grate* and *scrape*, *slice* and *separate* become incantations that bind the sensuality of food to memory. As other collectors seek rare books, elephant figurines, and vintage photographs, I treasure hunt for recipes so I may reproduce their power, so I'll know what they know—how to dazzle, nurture, sustain.

INITIATION

I knock on the kitchen door, fumbling over "recipe, borsht, please." In the soup served by my Polish host, Mrs. Gebala, beets spoke the soil's language of mineral and rain, not the familiar tongue of tin can. Mellow, magenta medallions floated in broth, slices of hard-earth hearts sweetened with cream. I felt as though I spoke the sound of zippers, but Mrs. Gebala understood.

Kitchen witches rarely perform for an audience; culinary spells work best when a person yields to the mystery of taste. Perhaps Mrs. Gebala felt sorry for me, the professor so far from home. She held two crimson beets in the air, pretended to slice them, scribbled "30" in my journal, and pointed to a pot. From the refrigerator to the stove, Mrs. Gebala strode with a lemon, carrot, and clove of garlic in hand. She added fresh-churned butter and cream, charade-style, to the empty pot. Sprigs of dill sprung like a bouquet from her sleeve. With a pinch of salt sprinkled in, she cast another spell: I believed I could mimic her magic.

SEDUCTION

"For the salad, select two *domates*—firm, red," Sezen Hanım said. *Domates*, I whispered, repeating the Turkish word. I pushed into the smooth skin, unsure how it would respond to the arrow-tipped blade. The tomato opened with little pressure and I arranged the heart-shaped slices on a plate.

"What's the word for 'heart'?" I asked.

"*Kalp*," she replied. *Kalp, kalp*. I committed it to memory. Sezen Hanım described those close to her own. I knew her husband from work, but she also had a son, Sunkar, my age.

"Sunkar is a doctor," Sezen Hanım said. "His job leaves him little time for social engagements. May I invite my family over for dinner after your next lesson?"

"Sure," I replied. *Sunkar, Sunkar, Sunkar.* "And what's next?"

"*Salatalık*," she said as she pulled three cucumbers out of a bag. "Peel like this." Her knife flashed; ribbons fell into the sink. While I diced them, Sezen Hanım minced parsley.

"Toss the vegetables with lemon juice," she said. I handed her a nipple-tipped lemon and she rolled it back and forth across the countertop before slicing it in half and squeezing four tablespoons into the salad. We added olive oil and salt. At my table, we took eager first bites of crisp vegetables and chewy bread. We ate slowly, the conversation ranging from our favorite books to our favorite desserts. We both pushed our plates away with satisfaction.

The next day Sunkar called. "Hi," he said. "I want to introduce myself. My mother was happy to meet you. She says you like to cook?" The spell of Turkish salad: seduction by proxy.

APPRENTICING

Sometimes recipes rely on a cook's experience, such as understanding the shade of green steamed broccoli achieves before turning mushy. Sometimes they assume a working knowledge, such as the difference between chop and dice. The most experienced spell-casters, like my Grandma Welby, perfected spells over time and make it seem easy. On any given Sunday afternoon of my childhood, I would scour her kitchen for peanut butter cups and milk; there wasn't much more besides jars of pickled pig's feet and Miracle Whip. Yet in a kitchen the size of an ample closet, she made meals: butter and bread, dill pickles, mashed potatoes and gravy, roast beef or pork, green beans, and pie. It seemed she could always make something from nothing.

To understand how she summoned all that food, I consumed recipes. At age eight, I labeled *Strawberry Shortcake's Cooking Fun* with days of the week for a menu; four decades later, I'm still collecting. I tape recipes onto index cards and gather food into albums of feasts: Heavenly Earth Burgers, Sesame Soba Noodle Salad, and Ratatouille in "Vegetarian Dishes;" Yellow Pepper, Egg Drop, Golden Winter, and Harvest Minestrone in "Soups;" Lemon Ginger Muffins and Scottish Oat Scones in "Breads." A recipe may ask me to coat a sauté pan with olive oil, apply heat, add onions and garlic, and cook until tender. Will I add peppers or celery next? Fennel or cumin? At each step, a recipe can move toward alchemy. Possibilities unfold when I blend one-fourth cup sugar with two-thirds cup butter and beat until fluffy, when three-quarters cup bittersweet cocoa is measured out and stirred in.

The best spell-casters learn from their mistakes. My sophomore year of high school, I picked through my mother's index cards until I selected a proper meal for a boyfriend: Shrimp and Wild Rice Casserole. I thawed the frozen shrimp, diced the onion, and cubed the Velveeta. To that I added Campbell's Condensed Mushroom Soup, butter, lemon juice, wild rice, and two tablespoons of ground pepper. That's right. Two. Tablespoons. Anyone with an appreciation for basic seasoning would know that "gr" in front of "pepper" meant something else. Sometimes kitchen witches muck up something, but the intention makes the recipe work anyway; sometimes, even the best spellcasting fails.

BAIT-AND-SWITCH

My mother used to can food on the stove, the overhead vent sucking up steam, the steel pressure cooker shaking and whistling like a living cauldron. She canned homegrown tomatoes for spaghetti sauce and she canned salmon that my father brought back from Canadian fishing trips. As a table sorceress who cooks from scratch, she uses time-tested—or friend-tested—spells to distract my father from his other love.

Once, my mother believed that if she plated the pot roast, potatoes, and carrots the second my father walked through the door after work, the aroma would make him forget about the Wild Turkey in the liquor cabinet. Or maybe a tender steak procured from the East Side Locker would be too filling—less space for a six-pack. Maybe the food would arrest an alcoholic's starvation. Maybe it would satisfy his roving hunger, a hunger so sharp his words become blades and so democratic that a simple phrase or facial expression could spark its urgency.

Perhaps Mom's spells gained potency over time. Perhaps they took decades to perfect. For the last couple of years, Dad drinks tea and Coke Zero, his words of support and love wrapping her like a hug.

SAFETY

In the mountain village of Çamlıyayla, Turkey, Feyza simmered tea in a samovar. Her brother, Ahmet, and I visited her to escape the sweltering city heat. On the table, she'd arranged a bowl of cherries, turning any blemish on a piece of fruit inward. I imagine her up high on the orchard ladder. Cherries tip the wrists of green-leafed branches, the twinned bulbs close to bursting. Thud, thud, thud. Pairs drop into the bucket. She plucks by touching the stems, not the fruit, so her hands won't look bruised. And they weren't when she served us tea. So where did I expect to see the marks her husband left? Everyone suspected. Ahmet's father had invited Feyza and her children to move into his home, but she hadn't gone.

Feyza appeared to do everything right. Around the wooden table, she tiptoed. Her hands didn't waver as she poured boiling tea into her husband's hourglass cup. Her four-year-old son grasped her hand when his father's gruff voice demanded cubes of sugar, but she didn't flinch. Plunk, plunk, plunk. With a baby secured to her hip by one hand, she stirred until the sugar dissolved with the other. Not a strand of hair escaped her headscarf.

Two years later, when I learned that Feyza had died at age twenty-six, I wondered when the spell failed to work. How can the magic of care and order dissipate bleeding in a brain?

GLAMOUR

My ex-husband's mother violated all spellcasting principles except one: the illusion. She'd unbox *pollo francesca*, *bisteac a la parilla*, and *pernil* from Styrofoam boxes that she'd brought home from Estrella del Caribbe, a restaurant she owned. Her brother-in-law, Jesus, did the actual cooking. Millie might sprinkle slices of mozzarella and tomato with vinaigrette, but otherwise she ironed a linen tablecloth and set the dining-room table for her four children and husband. In the kitchen, she'd scoop out *arroz blanco, arroz amarillo, moro, tostones, maduros* and *ceviche* onto her best china, bowls we traded around the candle-lit table. I always thought her spells lacked sparkle and strength because I knew her stovetop and counters were clean, her refrigerator packed with leftovers, not ingredients. I changed my mind when she died; her children never gathered around that table together again.

TRANSMUTATION

In a Polish farmhouse, Kasha dazzled me by transforming flowers into an elixir that conjured a long-forgotten memory. She stuffed a pot with twenty clusters of elderflower blossoms clipped from a bramble of asters, clover, purple comfrey, buttercups and roadside grasses. Like a forest sprite bent on mischief, Kasha swiveled between the stove and table of supplies: canisters of flour lined up against wrinkled wallpaper, fresh cream in a vase, eggs nestled in a basket. She tore open a paper bag and dumped in two kilos of sugar, grains cascading over the wire-thin stems like sand sliding from a plastic pail. Stirring with a wooden spoon, she poured in two liters of boiling water. The sugar and blossoms pinwheeled in the pot, heat extracting the tangy flavor. Was Kasha's bubbling laughter the key element in the transformation? After it cooled, she strained the elderflower-infused syrup and stirred in lemon juice. When its perfume wafted into my nose, I recalled plucking petals from purple thistles and sucking the sweetness from the white-tipped ends. When had I forgotten the recipe of wild simplicity? Kasha offered a brief toast to elderflower and we gulped summer into our throats.

EFFECTS

What makes cooking alchemy is the possibility of transforming common ingredients into valuable experiences. And the possibilities for surprise. As I survey the empty plates after my guests leave, I wonder about the effects of my spellcasting. I've practiced recipes long enough to know that I usually forego dazzle in favor of nurture. For this meal, I intended comfort, the essential atmosphere for good conversation. I planned for ease, eliminating recipes with distracting, pungent ingredients. Did I accomplish my goals? They smiled at the presentation. Between storytelling and jokes, we took second helpings of chicken-and-noodles, sopping broth up with buttered rolls. We left only crumbs of the generous pieces of cake. Over cups of tea, we laughed. I heard sighs of satisfaction as the meal concluded. This was one successful spell. Yet power can fall from the cook's hands as easily as spilled salt. The complex chemistries of vegetable and mineral mirror those of social interaction, and both can alter tastes and textures. So I'll continue to collect recipes and continue to cook, even though I'll never be able to completely account for what slips in the experience of food moving between plate and lips.

Flame & Wish

I DIDN'T KNOW THIS AS A CHILD, but I felt it: When someone lights a candle in prayer, their desire pierces the veil between worlds and the flame exists at the boundary. Let me light this for you.

Sent by my teacher to retrieve a missalette for religion class, I walked through the empty church until I stood before a bank of flickering wishes near the baptismal font. Tealights, votives, and pillars—wax as creamy white as my skin. Before the candles secured in red glass holders, I trembled. I felt eager to choose words, pick the candle, and usher the flame into existence under God's watchful eyes. Elderly women after Sunday mass usually dropped two quarters in the metal slot and lit a fresh wick with the flame of another. I was ten and faithful and wanted a congregation of flame.

I STOOD IN THE PEWS with the 7th grade, plaid-clad girls at St. Pius X. Stained glass, a fist thick and unevenly cut, cast a quilt of cerulean, ruby, and goldenrod on our heads as a box of candles passed down the row, slender sticks with flimsy wax-catchers near the bottom. With all the candles lit in the row, a surging fervor moved inside me. If I'd been born Pentecostal or Baptist, the Holy Spirit would've spurred me to the altar; I would've stood where my sister's casket stood a year earlier; I would've spoken in tongues and tears: "Move this burden of grief, Christ Jesus!" Zeal spun, my heart a dervish. How would God know my prayer without my words? In my *Lives of the Saints* book, St. Lucy's face radiated ecstatic energy; in one hand she held a palm branch, and in the other a dish upon which she'd placed her plucked-out eyes. In some stories, God restored her vision because she'd suffered in his name. My parents donated my sister's eyes to science. I dripped candlewax on my wrist and felt it sear my skin. God never spoke in that scar.

IN THE HILLS ABOVE EPHESUS IN TURKEY, visitors can find the stone building that John took Mary after Jesus died, a home where she lived out her years. My high school students at Tarsus American College asked me to chaperone their class trip to Ephesus. A simple shrine with pews at the back, my students—all Muslim—crowded to watch my ritual. As I walked to the marble altar that featured candles and a statue of Mary, I felt dozens of curious eyes on my back. Grief flickered in my chest. That's when I knew to move my desire from my body into the flame with my prayer.

    I put two coins in a plate and selected the candle: "Mary, Mother of God, pray for my grandmother, Mary Christine, as she finds her Lord and Savior, amen." I focused on desire, its sparks moving through my fingers and into the candle as two wicks touched. The flame expanded, glowing.

SO NOW YOU'VE LOST someone you love, and I tell you that I'll light a candle. Cream-colored. Vanilla-scented. Wick black and curled. I set it on the windowsill and stand before it, matchbox in my hands. I think of you, of your beloved, and I recall the kind of pain that swells inside, swells so much it sends your heart spinning. If you can't release, you'll combust. I strike the match and speak, "Let this flame wick away grief. Let it shine on the boundary. Let it be an ephemeral tether of love everlasting."

Acknowledgments

For grants and fellowships which provided time and support for work on these essays, I thank the Heller Center at the University of Colorado, Colorado Springs; the Kimmel Harding Nelson Center for the Arts in Nebraska City; and the Griffith Award Fund and Research/Scholarship Support Program at South Dakota State University, Brookings.

For feedback on earlier versions of these essays, I thank Rochelle L. Harris-Cox, Amber Jensen, Mary Woster Haug, Jamie Nagy, Marianne Zarzana, Heidi Czerwiec, Priscilla Long, Robert Root, and my creative writing students who, over the years, supplied stellar insight. I also appreciate mentors, colleagues, presses, and reading venues that have supported my work over the years. Special thanks to Sara Henning and Kimberly Verhines at Stephen F. Austin for championing this essay collection.

For their love and steadfast encouragement, I thank my parents, Terry and Sharon Stewart, my brother, Terrance Stewart, my husband, Brian Rex, and my sons, Holden and Xavier.

For their dedication to literature and support of my work, I thank the editors and staff of the following magazines in which some of these essays appeared:

"The Gnôsis Associated with Snakes," *Briar Cliff Review*
"Crucible of Dreams," *DreamTime Magazine*
"Once Upon a Tower," *So to Speak*
"A Study of Nuns, Light, and (Eventually) Love," *1966: A Journal of Creative Nonfiction*
"Culinary Alchemy," *poemmemoirstory*
"Disordered," *The Lindenwood Review*
"Marriage and Marble," *Blue Lyra Review: A Journal of Diverse Voices*
"Filaments of Prayer," *North American Review*

"Toward Intimate Spaces," *Watershed Review*

"Hike to the Black Madonna," *Shenandoah: The Washington and Lee
    University Review*

"Beyond Sound," *The Pinch*

"New Lens," *Shadowbox Magazine*

"Writer of Calendars," *North Dakota Quarterly*

"An Archeology for Secrets," *Briar Cliff Review*

"Kitchen Salsa," *LUMINA*

"The Work of Hands," *South Dakota Review*

About the author

CHRISTINE STEWART-NUÑEZ is the author of several collections of poetry, including *The Poet & The Architect* (2021), *Untrussed* (2016) and *Bluewords Greening* (2016) —winner of the 2018 Whirling Prize (literature of disability theme). Her creative nonfiction has appeared in *North American Review, Shenandoah,* and *The Pinch* among other magazines. Several essays have won awards, including a Notable Essay in *Best American Essays 2012*. Christine served as South Dakota's poet laureate from 2019-2021. She teaches in the women's and gender studies program at the University of Manitoba in Winnipeg.

CPSIA information can be obtained
at www.ICGtesting.com
Printed in the USA
BVHW091225011122
650797BV00002B/15

9 781622 889303